St. Louis de Montfort's Total Consecration to Jesus through Mary
New, Day-by-Day, Easier-to-Read Translation

ISBN-13: 978-1-950782-07-9 (Holy Water Books)

HOLY WATER BOOKS
At the unexpected horizons of the New Evangelization

HOLYWATERBOOKS

please check out our
other titles online at
www.holywaterbooks.com

Cover design by Holy Water Books

TOTAL CONSECRATION To JESUS Through MARY

St. Louis de Montfort

New translation by Scott L. Smith, Jr.

TABLE OF CONTENTS

Introduction 7

Overview of the Marian Consecration 9

12 Day Preparation 11

    Day 1 11

    Day 2 16

    Day 3 20

    Day 4 24

    Day 5 28

    Day 6 32

    Day 7 36

    Day 8 40

    Day 9 44

    Day 10 48

    Day 11 52

    Day 12 56

First Week 60

    Day 13 60

    Day 14 65

    Day 15 69

    Day 16 73

    Day 17 77

    Day 18 81

    Day 19 85

Second Week 89

Day 20 89

Day 21 94

Day 22 98

Day 23 102

Day 24 106

Day 25 110

Day 26 114

Third Week 118

Day 27 118

Day 28 123

Day 29 127

Day 30 131

Day 31 135

Day 32 140

Day 33 145

Day 34: Day of Consecration 150

After Consecration 156

Supplement: This Devotion at Holy Communion 158

Appendix I: Prayers Recited during the Consecration 162

Veni Creator 163

Ave Maris Stella 164

Magnificat 165

Glory Be 165

Litany of the Holy Ghost 166

Litany of the Blessed Virgin Mary (Litany of Loreto) 168

Litany of the Holy Name of Jesus 171

St. Louis de Montfort's Prayer to Mary 174

O Jesus living in Mary 176

Appendix II: How-To Guide for Reciting the Rosary 177

How to Pray the Rosary 178

Prayers Recited with Rosary 179

Mysteries of the Rosary 182

Rosary Prayers in Spanish 183

St. Louis de Montfort's
Total Consecration to Jesus through Mary

Introduction

"The Immaculate alone has from God the promise of victory over Satan. She seeks souls that will consecrate themselves entirely to her, that will become in her hands forceful instruments for the defeat of Satan and the spread of God's kingdom."

- St. Maximilian Kolbe

Saint Pope John Paul II was a major proponent of St. Louis de Montfort's *Total Consecration to Jesus through Mary.* In his apostolic letter, "Rosarium Virginis Mariae," the Pope noted that his personal motto "Totus Tuus" (Totally Yours) was inspired by the Total Consecration. Perhaps Totus Tuus might soon become your personal motto, too!

Saint Pope John Paul II also said that reading St. Louis de Montfort's *True Devotion to the Blessed Virgin Mary* marked a turning point in his life. He talked about this in an October 2000 address to the 8th International Mariological Colloquium in Rome. Saint Pope John Paul noted that, throughout his life, he had read and re-read St. Louis de Montfort's book. He noted the following:

> Then I understood that I could not exclude the Lord's Mother from my life without neglecting the will of God-Trinity, who willed to begin and fulfill the great mysteries of the history of salvation with the responsible and faithful collaboration of the humble handmaid of Nazareth.

Not long before becoming pope, Pope Francis urged the world to look towards Mary and the Holy Family for defense and protection, and to do so fervently.

He also promoted St. John Bosco's famous dream: devotion to Mary, along with the Eucharist, are the immovable anchors that will guide the Church on the path to heaven. Pope Francis has said "The Eucharist has been given to us so that our life, like that of Mary, can completely become a Magnificat."

Overview of the Marian Consecration

The next 33 days of prayers and readings are the preparation for your Act of Consecration. The 34th day will be your day of consecration.

St. Louis de Montfort divides the 33 days into different sections, each with its own prayers to complement brief daily readings from Sacred Scripture, *The Imitation of Christ* by Thomas à Kempis, and Montfort's own work, *True Devotion to the Blessed Virgin*. This is how the days will be divided:

- 12 Day Preparation – Days 1-12

   First comes a 12 day preparation period that consists of emptying oneself of the spirit of the world in penance and mortification. For these 12 days, we pray the Veni Creator, the Ave Maris Stella, the Magnificat, and the Glory Be.

- Week One – Days 13-19

   The first week focuses on offering up our prayers and devotions for the purpose of coming to understand ourselves and our sins. Humility is the key. For this week, we pray the Litany of the Holy Ghost, the Litany of Loreto, and the Ave Maris Stella.

- Week Two – Days 20-26

  During the second week, we ask the Holy Ghost to help us better understand the Blessed Virgin. We pray the Litany of the Holy Ghost, the Litany of Loreto, the Ave Maris Stellis, the prayer to Mary by St. Louis de Montfort. We also add 5 decades of the Holy Rosary each day for assistance.

- Week Three – Days 27-33

  During the third week, we seek to better understand Christ through meditation and the Litany of the Holy Ghost, the Ave Maris Stella, and the Litany of the Holy Name of Jesus, Montfort's prayer to Jesus, and the prayer, O Jesus Living in Mary.

- Consecration Day – Day 34

Don't just read the readings, internalize them. Don't let your lips just mouth the prayers; truly pray them. Just saying the words won't work; it's not a magic incantation.

You may feel less motivated or less focused some days, but persevere. You may even miss a day. Keep going. Keep trying.

12 Day Preparation

Prayers said daily during the consecration are provided in Appendix I and II at the end of the text.

Day 1

Examine your conscience, pray, and practice renouncement of your own will. This mortification results in purity of heart.

This purity is the indispensable condition for contemplating God in heaven, to see Him on earth and to know Him by the light of faith. The first part of the preparation should be employed in casting off the spirit of the world which is contrary to that of Jesus Christ. The spirit of the world consists essentially in the denial of the supreme dominion of God. This denial is manifested in practice by sin and disobedience. Thus, it is principally opposed to the spirit of Christ, which is also that of Mary.

It manifests itself by the concupiscence of the flesh, by the concupiscence of the eyes, and by the pride of life, and by disobedience to God's laws and the abuse of created things. Its works are the following: sin in all forms, then all else by which the devil leads to sin; works which bring error and darkness to the mind, and seduction and corruption to the will. Its pomps are the splendor and the charms employed by the devil to render sin alluring in persons, places, and things.

Reading: The Gospel of Matthew 5:1-19

And seeing the multitudes, he went up into a mountain, and when he was set down, his disciples came unto him. And opening his mouth, he taught them, saying:

Blessed are the poor in spirit: for theirs is the kingdom of heaven.
Blessed are the meek: for they shall possess the land.
Blessed are they that mourn: for they shall be comforted.
Blessed are they that hunger and thirst after justice: for they shall have their fill.
Blessed are the merciful: for they shall obtain mercy.
Blessed are the clean of heart: for they shall see God.
Blessed are the peacemakers: for they shall be called children of God.
Blessed are they that suffer persecution for justice' sake: for theirs is the kingdom of heaven.
Blessed are ye when they shall revile you, and persecute you, and speak all that is evil against you, untruly, for my sake: Be glad and rejoice, for your reward is very great in heaven. For so they persecuted the prophets that were before you.

You are the salt of the earth. But if the salt lose its savour, wherewith shall it be salted? It is good for nothing any more but to be cast out, and to be trodden on by men. You are the light of the world. A city seated on a mountain cannot be hid. Neither do men light a candle and put it under a bushel, but upon a candlestick, that it may shine to all that are in the house. So let your light shine before men, that they may see your good works, and glorify your Father who is in heaven.

Do not think that I am come to destroy the law, or the prophets. I am not come to destroy, but to fulfill. For amen I say unto you, till heaven and earth pass, one jot, or one tittle shall not pass of the law, till all be fulfilled. He therefore that shall break one of these least commandments, and shall so teach men, shall be called the least in the kingdom of heaven. But he that shall do and teach, he shall be called great in the kingdom of heaven.

Daily Prayers to Recite: Veni Creator, Ave Maris Stella, Magnificat, and Glory Be (see text of prayers at Appendix I)

Journal Entry:

Here are some sample questions to get you started:

- What feelings, reactions, intuitions, desires, emotions, thoughts, or insights did you encounter in prayer?
- What word, phrase, image, or memory meant most to you during prayer?
- Is there something happening in my life that is becoming part of my prayer?
- Do I feel moved to do something concrete in my life?

ST. LOUIS DE MONTFORT

ST. Louis de Montfort

Day 2

Reading: The Gospel of Matthew 5:48, 6:1-15

Jesus said: "You, therefore, must be perfect, as your heavenly Father is perfect."

"Beware of practicing your piety before men in order to be seen by them; for then you will have no reward from your Father who is in heaven."

"Thus, when you give alms, sound no trumpet before you, as the hypocrites do in the synagogues and in the streets, that they may be praised by men. Truly, I say to you, they have their reward. But when you give alms, do not let your left hand know what your right hand is doing, so that your alms may be in secret; and your Father who sees in secret will reward you."

"And when you pray, you must not be like the hypocrites; for they love to stand and pray in the synagogues and at the street corners, that they may be seen by men. Truly, I say to you, they have their reward. But when you pray, go into your room and shut the door and pray to your Father who is in secret; and your Father who sees in secret will reward you."

"And in praying do not heap up empty phrases as the Gentiles do; for they think that they will be heard for their many words. Do not be like them, for your Father knows what you need before you ask him. Pray then like this:

Our Father who art in heaven, hallowed be thy name.
Thy kingdom come, Thy will be done, on earth as it is in heaven.
Give us this day our daily bread;
And forgive us our debts,
    As we also have forgiven our debtors;

And lead us not into temptation,
But deliver us from evil."

"For if you forgive men their trespasses, your heavenly Father also will forgive you; but if you do not forgive men their trespasses, neither will your Father forgive your trespasses."

"And when you fast, do not look dismal, like the hypocrites, for they disfigure their faces that their fasting may be seen by men. Truly, I say to you, they have their reward. But when you fast, anoint your head and wash your face, that your fasting may not be seen by men but by your Father who is in secret; and your Father who sees in secret will reward you."

Daily Prayers to Recite: Veni Creator, Ave Maris Stella, Magnificat, and Glory Be (see text of prayers at Appendix I)

Journal Entry:
Here are some sample questions to get you started:
- What feelings, reactions, intuitions, desires, emotions, thoughts, or insights did you encounter in prayer?
- What word, phrase, image, or memory meant most to you during prayer?
- Is there something happening in my life that is becoming part of my prayer?
- Do I feel moved to do something concrete in my life?

_____

_____

_____

_____

_____

_____

ST. LOUIS DE MONTFORT

_____

_____

_____

_____

_____

_____

_____

_____

_____

_____

_____

_____

_____

_____

_____

_____

_____

_____

_____

_____

_____

_____

_____

_____
_____
_____
_____
_____
_____
_____
_____
_____
_____
_____
_____
_____
_____
_____
_____
_____
_____
_____
_____
_____
_____
_____
_____
_____
_____
_____

DAY 3

Reading: The Gospel of Matthew 7:1-14

Jesus said: "Judge not, that you be not judged. For with the judgment you pronounce you will be judged, and the measure you give will be the measure you get. Why do you see the speck that is in your brother's eye, but do not notice the log that is in your own eye? Or how can you say to your brother, 'Let me take the speck out of your eye,' when there is the log in your own eye? You hypocrite, first take the log out of your own eye, and then you will see clearly to take the speck out of your brother's eye."

"Do not give dogs what is holy; and do not throw your pearls before swine, lest they trample them under foot and turn to attack you."

"Ask, and it will be given you; seek, and you will find; knock, and it will be opened to you. For every one who asks receives, and he who seeks finds, and to him who knocks it will be opened. Or what man of you, if his son asks him for bread, will give him a stone? Or if he asks for a fish, will give him a serpent? If you then, who are evil, know how to give good gifts to your children, how much more will your Father who is in heaven give good things to those who ask him! So whatever you wish that men would do to you, do so to them; for this is the law and the prophets."

"Enter by the narrow gate; for the gate is wide and the way is easy, that leads to destruction, and those who enter by it are many. For the gate is narrow and the way is hard, that leads to life, and those who find it are few."

Daily Prayers to Recite: Veni Creator, Ave Maris Stella, Magnificat, and Glory Be (see text of prayers at Appendix I)

Journal Entry:

Here are some sample questions to get you started:

- What feelings, reactions, intuitions, desires, emotions, thoughts, or insights did you encounter in prayer?
- What word, phrase, image, or memory meant most to you during prayer?
- Is there something happening in my life that is becoming part of my prayer?
- Do I feel moved to do something concrete in my life?

_____

_____

_____

_____

_____

_____

_____

_____

_____

_____

_____

_____

_____

_____

_____

_____

_____

_____

ST. LOUIS DE MONTFORT

DAY 4

Reading: *Imitation of Christ* by Thomas á Kempis, Book III, Chapters 7, 40

That man has no good of himself, that he cannot glory in anything, Lord, what is man, that You are mindful of him? Or the son of man, that You visit him? What has man deserved that You should give him grace? Lord, what cause have I to complain, if You forsake me? Or what can I justly accuse, if You do not grant my petitions?

I may truly think and say this most assuredly: Lord I am nothing. I can do nothing by myself that is good. I am in all things defective and ever tend to nothing. Unless I am assisted and interiorly instructed by You, I become wholly tepid and relaxed. But You, O Lord, are unchanging and endure unto eternity. You are ever good, just and holy, doing all things well, justly, holily, and wisely.

But I am changing, having failed so many times, and am more inclined to go back, than to go forward. But, if You please, when You stretch out Your helping hand, it quickly becomes better. For You alone, far beyond the help of any man, can assist me and so strengthen me. Nothing so changes my demeanor and converts my heart, as the rest I find in You alone.

He who is too secure in time of peace is often too dejected in time of war. If you could just remember yourself as humble and little, and if you could keep your spirit ordered, you would not fall so easily into danger and offense. It is wise to remember: when you make your plans in the fervor of summertime, how it will be when the light is withdrawn.

Daily Prayers to Recite: Veni Creator, Ave Maris Stella, Magnificat, and Glory Be (see text of prayers at Appendix I)

Journal Entry:

Here are some sample questions to get you started:

- What feelings, reactions, intuitions, desires, emotions, thoughts, or insights did you encounter in prayer?
- What word, phrase, image, or memory meant most to you during prayer?
- Is there something happening in my life that is becoming part of my prayer?
- Do I feel moved to do something concrete in my life?

_____

_____

_____

_____

_____

_____

_____

_____

_____

_____

_____

_____

_____

_____

_____

_____

ST. LOUIS DE MONTFORT

Day 5

Reading: *Imitation of Christ* by Thomas á Kempis, Book III, Chapters 7, 40

If only I could cast from myself all human comfort. I would flee comfort either for the sake of devotion, or because nothing else can comfort me and I am compelled to seek You. Then, I might deservedly hope for Your favor and rejoice in the gift of a new consolation.

As often as it happens, I will give thanks to God from Whom all things proceed. Because, try as I might, I am but vanity and nothing in Your sight. I am an inconstant and weak man. I cannot glory in myself and on what basis, should I desire to be thought of highly? Only perhaps my very nothingness, and even this is most vain.

Such vanity is an evil plague, because it distracts us from true glory and robs us of heavenly grace. For, while a man takes complacency in himself, he displeases You. While he wants for human applause, he is deprived of true virtues.

True glory and holy exultation is to glory in You, and not in one's self. True glory is to rejoice in Your Name, but not in one's own strength. To find pleasure in no creature, except for Your sake.

Let Your Name be praised, not mine. Let Your work be magnified, not mine. Let Your Holy Name be blessed, but let me not seek the praise of men. You are my glory. You are the praise of my heart. In You, I will glory and rejoice forever; but for myself, I will glory in nothing but in my infirmities.

Daily Prayers to Recite: Veni Creator, Ave Maris Stella, Magnificat, and Glory Be (see text of prayers at Appendix I)

Journal Entry:

Here are some sample questions to get you started:

- What feelings, reactions, intuitions, desires, emotions, thoughts, or insights did you encounter in prayer?
- What word, phrase, image, or memory meant most to you during prayer?
- Is there something happening in my life that is becoming part of my prayer?
- Do I feel moved to do something concrete in my life?

_____

_____

_____

_____

_____

_____

_____

_____

_____

_____

_____

_____

_____

_____

_____

_____

_____

_____

ST. LOUIS DE MONTFORT

DAY 6

Reading: *Imitation of Christ* by Thomas á Kempis, Book I, Chapters 18

Look upon the bold examples of the Saints. Real perfection in the religious life shines in their lives. And you will see how little, almost nothing, that we do nowadays compares with them.

What are our lives compared with theirs? Saints and friends of Christ, they served our Lord in hunger and in thirst, in cold, in nakedness, in labor and in weariness, in watching and waiting, in fasting, prayers and holy meditations, and in frequent persecutions and reproaches.

How many terrible tribulations did the Apostles suffer? And the Martyrs, Confessors, Virgins, and all the rest who resolved to follow in the steps of Christ! They willingly offered their lives in this world, that they might have life everlasting.

What a strict and self-renouncing life, the Desert Fathers led! What long and grievous temptations they bore! To think how often were they harassed by the Devil, how frequent and fervent were the prayers they offered to God, and what rigorous abstinence they practiced.

Think how valiantly they battled to subdue their imperfections. Think how pure was their dedication to God. They labored by day and spent most of the night in prayer. Even while they labored, their minds were at prayer. They spent all their time profitably. Every hour seemed short when spent with God.

They forgot even basic bodily needs in the great sweetness of contemplation. They renounced all riches, dignities, honors, and kindred, taking hardly even what was necessary for life. It grieved them to serve the body even in its necessity. Accordingly, they were poor in earthly things, but very rich in grace and virtues.

Daily Prayers to Recite: Veni Creator, Ave Maris Stella, Magnificat, and Glory Be (see text of prayers at Appendix I)

Journal Entry:

Here are some sample questions to get you started:

- What feelings, reactions, intuitions, desires, emotions, thoughts, or insights did you encounter in prayer?
- What word, phrase, image, or memory meant most to you during prayer?
- Is there something happening in my life that is becoming part of my prayer?
- Do I feel moved to do something concrete in my life?

ST. LOUIS DE MONTFORT

DAY 7

Reading: *Imitation of Christ* by Thomas á Kempis, Book I, Chapters 18 continued

Outwardly, the Desert Fathers suffered want. Inwardly, they were refreshed with grace and Divine consolation. To the world, they were aliens and strange and despised. To God, they were dear and beloved friends.

In them shined all the perfection of virtue: they persevered in true humility. They lived in simple obedience. They walked in charity and patience. And so, every day they advanced in spirit and gained great grace with God. They are an example to all religious people. Their lives should stir us all to devotion. Their example should excite us to grow in grace and virtue. It should not be the example of the lukewarm, the dissolute, and the idle that we follow into vice and distraction.

How great was the fervor of the early religious fathers while still in the dawn of Christianity and the beginning of monasticism! How great was their devotion in prayer, and their zeal for virtue. How great was the discipline, reverence, and obedience that flourished under the rule of their superiors. Their deeds still bear witness to this day that they, who battled for holiness and perfection, trampled the world beneath their feet.

Nowadays, all it takes for a man to be considered great and virtuous is to avoid public shame. To be exceptional, a man needs only to keep a little spark of his original fervor alive. A memory of a conversion is enough, when it is ongoing conversion which is so desperately needed. How lukewarm and pitiful is our current state! How quickly we fall away after that retreat or mountaintop experience. We grow tried with our lives because of sloth and meekness. Out of negligence, we let the fire of God's magnificence grow stale. Just think of how we must afflict Jesus, who has seen so often, and even in us, the fire of the great saints.

Daily Prayers to Recite: Veni Creator, Ave Maris Stella, Magnificat, and Glory Be (see text of prayers at Appendix I)

Journal Entry:

Here are some sample questions to get you started:

- What feelings, reactions, intuitions, desires, emotions, thoughts, or insights did you encounter in prayer?
- What word, phrase, image, or memory meant most to you during prayer?
- Is there something happening in my life that is becoming part of my prayer?
- Do I feel moved to do something concrete in my life?

_____

_____

_____

_____

_____

_____

_____

_____

_____

_____

_____

_____

_____

_____

ST. LOUIS DE MONTFORT

DAY 8

Reading: *Imitation of Christ* by Thomas á Kempis, Book I, Chapters 13

For as long as we live in this world, temptations and tribulations will be our constant companions. As it is written in Job, "Man's life on earth is a temptation." Otherwise translated, "Man's life on earth is warfare." This war requires that every man be on guard about his temptations and watchful in prayer. Or else, the devil, who never sleeps but is always prowling about and seeking to devour, will deceive him and catch him.

No man is so perfect and holy as to be wholly free of temptation. Nevertheless, temptations are very profitable to man *when we wrestle with them*. Though troublesome and painful they may be, temptations humble, purify, and instruct us. All the Saints who now wear crowns in Heaven wrestled through many tribulations and temptations and were purified by them. Those who surrendered, who could not bear to wrestle with their temptations, fell away and are now Hell's prisoners.

Many seek to flee temptations, and fall worse into them. Instead of cleaving to Christ, they fall into the devil's embrace. This battle cannot be won by fleeing the battlefield. Only with patience and true humility, we overcome our enemies.

A man gains little profit by merely fleeing the outward occasions of sin. He must pluck pluck out the root, the disordered desires hidden away in our hearts. Like weeds, temptations will come back again and again, growing in strength each time. Little by little, however, with patience, fortitude, and God's grace, you will sooner overcome temptations than by relying on your own strength and gritted teeth.

In your temptation, take counsel with an accountability partner or spiritual director. These should not deal harshly with one who is tempted. Instead, they should pour out consolation and comfort, just as they would want to be comforted.

The beginning of all temptations is inconstancy of mind and too little confidence in God. Just as a ship, without rudder or helm, will be driven off course by every storm, so the man who neglects his resolutions will soon lose sight of his guiding star when buffeted by waves of temptation.

Daily Prayers to Recite: Veni Creator, Ave Maris Stella, Magnificat, and Glory Be (see text of prayers at Appendix I)

Journal Entry:
Here are some sample questions to get you started:
- What feelings, reactions, intuitions, desires, emotions, thoughts, or insights did you encounter in prayer?
- What word, phrase, image, or memory meant most to you during prayer?
- Is there something happening in my life that is becoming part of my prayer?
- Do I feel moved to do something concrete in my life?

_____

_____

_____

_____

_____

_____

ST. LOUIS DE MONTFORT

DAY 9

Reading: *Imitation of Christ* by Thomas á Kempis, Book I, Chapter 13 continued

Fire purifies gold, and temptation purifies the righteous man. We often do not know what we are capable of. Temptation, however, shows us plainly.

We must be watchful, especially at the beginning of a temptation. It is then that the enemy is most easily overcome. We cannot let the devil enter the door of the mind. We must hold him back at the threshold the very moment he knocks. As the saying goes, "Resist beginnings; all too late the cure."

First comes an unclean thought into the mind. Then comes a strong phantasm of imagination. Delight and pleasure follow, and then various evil motions. By the end, there is full consent. So, little by little, the devil gains entrance, if he is not resisted in the beginning. The slower a man is to resist, the weaker his resistance becomes, and the devil is daily stronger against him.

Some suffer grievous temptations in the beginning of their conversion, and some suffer at the end. Some are troubled nearly their whole life, and some are only ever tempted very lightly. This is all according to the wisdom and equity of God. God weighs each man's condition and merits and ordains all things for the salvation of His elect.

Therefore, we must not despair when we are tempted. Instead, pray all the more fervently to God that in his infinite goodness and fatherly pity, he will help us overcome every temptation. God will, as St. Paul said, go before us in grace, so we are able to withstand the temptation.

Let us, then, humble ourselves under the strong hand of Almighty God in every temptation. God will save and exalt those who are meek and humble in spirit. For again, a man is proven in temptation, as is the progress he has made. His merit shines before God and his virtue is made manifest.

Daily Prayers to Recite: Veni Creator, Ave Maris Stella, Magnificat, and Glory Be (see text of prayers at Appendix I)

Journal Entry:

Here are some sample questions to get you started:

- What feelings, reactions, intuitions, desires, emotions, thoughts, or insights did you encounter in prayer?
- What word, phrase, image, or memory meant most to you during prayer?
- Is there something happening in my life that is becoming part of my prayer?
- Do I feel moved to do something concrete in my life?

ST. LOUIS DE MONTFORT

_____

_____

_____

_____

_____

_____

_____

_____

_____

_____

_____

_____

_____

_____

_____

_____

_____

_____

_____

_____

_____

_____

_____

_____

_____

DAY 10

Reading: *Imitation of Christ* by Thomas á Kempis, Book III, Chapter 10, "That it is sweet to forsake the world and to serve God"

I will speak again to you, my Lord Jesus, and I will not be silent. I will speak into the ears of my Lord, my God and my King, Who is on high:

How great is Your sweetness, O Lord, which You have hidden for those that fear You! But what are You to those who love You? What are You to those who serve You with their whole heart? Truly, it is the unspeakable sweetness of contemplation, which You have bestowed on those who love You.

In this most of all, You have showed me the sweetness of Your love, that when I had no being, You made me. And when I was straying far from You, You brought me back again, that I might serve You. And You have commanded me to serve You.

Fountain of everlasting love, what shall I say of You? How can I forget You, Who remembered me even after I was dead and lost? Beyond all hope, You showed mercy to Your servant. Without deserving it, You gave me Your mercy and friendship. But what can I give you in return for such gifts?

Not all men are granted leave to forsake all things, to renounce the world, and to live a solitary, monastic life. Is it much that I should serve You, when all of creation is bound to do the same? It doesn't seem like much to serve You. What does seem extraordinary is that You would receive such a wretched and unworthy man as me into your service.

It is a great honor and a great glory to serve You and despise all things for You. Those who willingly subject themselves to

Your holy service will receive great grace. Those who cast aside all carnal pleasures out of love for You will experience the Holy Spirit and the sweetest of consolations.

Daily Prayers to Recite: Veni Creator, Ave Maris Stella, Magnificat, and Glory Be (see text of prayers at Appendix I)

Journal Entry:

Here are some sample questions to get you started:
- What feelings, reactions, intuitions, desires, emotions, thoughts, or insights did you encounter in prayer?
- What word, phrase, image, or memory meant most to you during prayer?
- Is there something happening in my life that is becoming part of my prayer?
- Do I feel moved to do something concrete in my life?

_____

_____

_____

_____

_____

_____

_____

_____

_____

_____

_____

_____

_____

ST. LOUIS DE MONTFORT

DAY 11

Reading: *Imitation of Christ* by Thomas á Kempis, Book I, Chapter 25, "On the Fervent Amendment of our Whole Life"

There was once an anxious man, who often wavered between hope and fear and doubted whether he was in a state of grace. The man threw himself to the ground in prayer before one of the altars in the church and said "Oh, if I only knew if I will persevere in virtue until my death."

That very instant the man heard within him a heavenly answer: "And if you did know this, what would you do? Do now what you would do then, and you will be saved."

The man was immediately comforted and he committed himself wholly to the Divine Will. From then on, his anxious thoughts ceased. His curiosity no longer dwelled over what would happen to him. Instead, he spent his energy discerning God's will for his life. He sought to begin and end each of his deeds to the pleasure of God.

"Trust in the Lord and do good deeds," says the Prophet David. "Inhabit the land, and you shall feed from its riches."

There is one thing in particular that stops many men from progressing in the spiritual life and amending their lives. It is the false worldly fear of the pain and labor which is needed in the struggle to win virtue. Those who strive the most manfully to overcome their most difficult vices will most quickly advance in virtue. A man profits most and wins the most grace when he tackles those things in which he most has to overcome himself.

All men do not, indeed, have equal difficulties to overcome. Some men have greater passions than others. Nevertheless, a zealous lover of God, even if he has stronger passions, will also make a stronger advance in virtue. The man of great passion will make greater progress than he of little passion, who is less fervent toward virtue.

Two things greatly help a man amend his life: (1) a strong withdrawal from himself and from those things which his body most craves, and (2) a fervent labor for the virtues he most needs.

Daily Prayers to Recite: Veni Creator, Ave Maris Stella, Magnificat, and Glory Be (see text of prayers at Appendix I)

Journal Entry:
Here are some sample questions to get you started:
- What feelings, reactions, intuitions, desires, emotions, thoughts, or insights did you encounter in prayer?
- What word, phrase, image, or memory meant most to you during prayer?
- Is there something happening in my life that is becoming part of my prayer?
- Do I feel moved to do something concrete in my life?

_____

_____

_____

_____

_____

_____

_____

_____

ST. LOUIS DE MONTFORT

Day 12

Reading: *Imitation of Christ* by Thomas á Kempis, Book I, Chapter 25, continued

Work especially to overcome those vices in yourself, which most disturb you in others. Wherever you go, profit from the example of others. When you observe virtuous examples, emulate them. When you observe vicious examples, avoid them. As you consider the work of others, remember also that your works, too, are being observed.

How sweet and pleasing it is, to see our brothers who fervent and devout, obedient and well-taught. How sad and grievous it is, to see our brothers who walk disordered paths, not applying themselves to that for which they are made. How hurtful it is, to see our brothers neglect their calling and neglect those who have been entrusted to their care, and set their minds to what is forbidden.

Be mindful of the purpose that has been set before you. Set always before you the image of Christ Crucified. If you lovingly behold Jesus' afflicted face, you may well be ashamed. Ashamed that you have not better conformed your life to His, despite all the time you have been on the way of God.

A man should inwardly and seriously exercise himself in the most holy life and passion of our Lord. He will find there abundantly all he needs. Neither will he need to seek anywhere else, apart from Jesus. If only Jesus crucified were more often in our hearts and minds, how quickly we would be filled with everything we need. A fervent and diligent man is thus prepared for all things and cheerfully obedient to all God's commands.

Resisting vices and temptations is harder work than the toil and sweat of physical labor. A man who does not fight the little sins, little by little, will fall into the greater sins. You will always rejoice in the evening, if you have spent your day profitably avoiding and conquering sin.

Be watchful of yourself. Stir yourself up for devotion. Admonish yourself against sin and ruin. And whatever you do for others, do not forget to do for yourself. The more violently you fight against your own will and for God's will, the more you will advance in virtue.

Daily Prayers to Recite: Veni Creator, Ave Maris Stella, Magnificat, and Glory Be (see text of prayers at Appendix I)

Journal Entry:
Here are some sample questions to get you started:
- What feelings, reactions, intuitions, desires, emotions, thoughts, or insights did you encounter in prayer?
- What word, phrase, image, or memory meant most to you during prayer?
- Is there something happening in my life that is becoming part of my prayer?
- Do I feel moved to do something concrete in my life?

_____

_____

_____

_____

_____

_____

_____

_____

ST. LOUIS DE MONTFORT

FIRST WEEK

DAY 13

Theme for the Week: Knowledge of Self

All that you do this week: prayers, examinations, reflection, acts of renouncing our own will, acts of contrition for our sins, acts of contempt of self. All these should be performed at the feet of Mary.

Imagine yourself putting all these things at Mary's precious feet. We pray that we will come to know ourselves in her light, who is the immaculate reflection of Jesus. Near her, we will be able to behold the abyss of our miseries without despairing.

All our pious actions should be directed to a special request: *for a knowledge of ourselves and for contrition for our sins, and that we should do and receive all this in a spirit of piety.* During this period, we will focus not so much on the opposition between the spirit of Jesus and our own. Rather, we pray to grasp fully the miserable and humiliating state to which our sins have reduced us.

The True Devotion to Mary is an easy, short, sure, and perfect way to arrive at complete and perfect union with Our Lord Jesus. Nevertheless, to enter seriously upon this path, we need to be strongly convinced of the misery caused by our sins and our own helplessness. This is why we must attain this knowledge of ourselves.

Reading: The Gospel of Luke, 11:1-10

He was praying in a certain place, and when he ceased, one of his disciples said to him, "Lord, teach us to pray, as John taught his disciples." And he said to them, "When you pray, say:

> Father, hallowed be thy name. Thy kingdom come. Give us each day our daily bread; and forgive us our sins, for we ourselves forgive everyone who is indebted to us; and lead us not into temptation.

And he said to them, "Which of you who has a friend will go to him at midnight and say to him, 'Friend, lend me three loaves; for a friend of mine has arrived on a journey, and I have nothing to set before him'; and he will answer from within, 'Do not bother me; the door is now shut, and my children are with me in bed; I cannot get up and give you anything'? I tell you, though he will not get up and give him anything because he is his friend, yet because of his importunity he will rise and give him whatever he needs."

"And I tell you, Ask, and it will be given you; seek, and you will find; knock, and it will be opened to you. For every one who asks receives, and he who seeks finds, and to him who knocks it will be opened."

"What father among you, if his son asks for a fish, will instead of a fish give him a serpent; or if he asks for an egg, will give him a scorpion? If you then, who are evil, know how to give good gifts to your children, how much more will the heavenly Father give the Holy Spirit to those who ask him!"

Daily Prayers to Recite: Litany of the Holy Ghost, Litany of the Blessed Virgin Mary, and Ave Maris Stella (see text of prayers at Appendix I)

Journal Entry:

Here are some sample questions to get you started:

- What feelings, reactions, intuitions, desires, emotions, thoughts, or insights did you encounter in prayer?
- What word, phrase, image, or memory meant most to you during prayer?
- Is there something happening in my life that is becoming part of my prayer?
- Do I feel moved to do something concrete in my life?

_____

_____

_____

_____

_____

_____

_____

_____

_____

_____

_____

_____

_____

_____

_____

_____

_____

ST. LOUIS DE MONTFORT

DAY 14

Reading: *Imitation of Christ* by Thomas á Kempis, Book III, Chapter 13, "Of the Obedience of One in Humble Subjection, After the Example of Jesus Christ"

My son, says the Lord Jesus Christ, he who endeavors to withdraw himself from obedience, withdraws himself from grace, cf. Matt. 16:24. He who seeks possessions for himself, loses those which is given to all.

If a man doesn't cheerfully and freely submit himself to his superior, it is a sign that his flesh is not yet perfectly obedient to him. Such a man's flesh kicks and murmurs against him. Therefore, if you truly desire to overcome yourself and make your flesh obedient to your spirit, learn first to obey you superiors.

The outward enemy is sooner overcome if the inner man – the soul – is not feeble and weak. There is no greater or more troublesome enemy to the soul than *you*, if your flesh is not in harmony with your spirit. You must, therefore, develop a contempt for yourself, if you desire to prevail against your flesh and blood. To the same degree you love yourself inordinately, you will fear to resign yourself to another's will.

Is it so great a matter for a man, who is but dust from nothing, to subject himself to another for God's sake, when I, the Almighty and the Most High God, who created all things from nothing, humbly subjected Myself to man for your sake? I made myself the humblest and lowest of all men (Luke 2:7; John 13:14), that you might overcome your pride with My humility.

O dust! Learn to be obedient. Learn to humble yourself, who are but earth and clay. Learn to bow down under the feet of all men for My sake. Learn to break your will and to be subject to all from the heart.

Daily Prayers to Recite: Litany of the Holy Ghost, Litany of the Blessed Virgin Mary, and Ave Maris Stella (see text of prayers at Appendix I)

Journal Entry:

Here are some sample questions to get you started:

- What feelings, reactions, intuitions, desires, emotions, thoughts, or insights did you encounter in prayer?
- What word, phrase, image, or memory meant most to you during prayer?
- Is there something happening in my life that is becoming part of my prayer?
- Do I feel moved to do something concrete in my life?

_____

_____

_____

_____

_____

_____

_____

_____

_____

_____

_____

_____

_____

ST. LOUIS DE MONTFORT

DAY 15

Reading 1: Luke 13:1-5, "Repent or Perish"

There were some present at that very time who told him of the Galileans whose blood Pilate had mingled with their sacrifices. And he answered them, "Do you think that these Galileans were worse sinners than all the other Galileans, because they suffered thus? I tell you, No; but unless you repent you will all likewise perish. Or those eighteen upon whom the tower in Silo'am fell and killed them, do you think that they were worse offenders than all the others who dwelt in Jerusalem? I tell you, No; but unless you repent you will all likewise perish."

Reading 2: *True Devotion to the Blessed Virgin Mary*, Nos. 81 and 82, "We Need Mary in order to Die to Ourselves"

Secondly, in order to empty ourselves of self, we must die daily to ourselves. This involves our renouncing what the powers of the soul and the senses of the body incline us to do. We must see as if we did not see, hear as if we did not hear, and use the things of this world as if we did not use them.

This is what St. Paul calls "dying daily". Unless the grain of wheat falls to the ground and dies, it remains only a single grain and does not bear any good fruit. We must die to self and our holiest devotions must lead us to this necessary and fruitful death. Otherwise, we shall not bear fruit of any worth and our devotions will cease to be profitable. All our good works will be tainted by self-love and self-will. Our greatest sacrifices and our best actions, then, will be unacceptable to God.

Consequently, when we die, we shall find ourselves devoid of virtue and merit. We will discover that we do not possess even one spark of that pure love which God shares only with those who have died to themselves and whose life is hidden within Jesus Christ.

Thirdly, we must choose among all the devotions to the Blessed Virgin the one which will lead us more surely to this dying to self. This devotion will be the best and the most sanctifying for us.

Daily Prayers to Recite: Litany of the Holy Ghost, Litany of the Blessed Virgin Mary, and Ave Maris Stella (see text of prayers at Appendix I)

Journal Entry:

Here are some sample questions to get you started:
- What feelings, reactions, intuitions, desires, emotions, thoughts, or insights did you encounter in prayer?
- What word, phrase, image, or memory meant most to you during prayer?
- Is there something happening in my life that is becoming part of my prayer?
- Do I feel moved to do something concrete in my life?

_____

_____

_____

_____

_____

_____

_____

_____

_____

ST. LOUIS DE MONTFORT

DAY 16

Reading 1: *True Devotion To the Blessed Virgin Mary*, No. 228, "Preparatory Exercises"

During the first week, we offered up all our prayers and acts of devotion to acquire knowledge of ourselves and sorrow for our sins. We are to perform all our actions in a spirit of humility. With this end in view, we may, if we wish, meditate on what St. Louis de Montfort has said concerning our corrupted nature, and consider ourselves during six days of the week as nothing but sails, slugs, toads, swine, snakes, and goats.

Or else, we may meditate on the following three considerations of St. Bernard: "Remember what you were: corrupted seed.
Remember what you are: a body destined for decay.
Remember what you will be: food for worms."

Ask our Lord and the Holy Spirit to enlighten you saying, "Lord, that I may see," or "Lord, let me know myself," or "Come, Holy Spirit." Every day we should say the "Litany of the Holy Spirit." We will then turn to our Blessed Lady and beg her to obtain for us that great grace which is the foundation of all others, the grace of self-knowledge. For this intention, we will say each day the "Ave Maris Stella" and the "Litany of the Blessed Virgin."

Reading 2: *Imitation of Christ* by Thomas á Kempis, Book II, Chapter 5, "Of Self-consideration"

We cannot trust in ourselves or in our intelligence too much, because we often lacking in grace and understanding, c.f. Jer. 17:5. Precious little light is there in us, and too often we lose this through neglect. We do not see or even want to see just how blind we are. Oftentimes we do evil and then try to defend ourselves, doing even greater harm, c.f. Psalm 141:4.

Sometimes, too, we are moved with passion and mistake it as zeal from God. We passionately admonish small faults in our neighbors and ignore far greater faults in ourselves, c.f. Matt. 7:5. We may ruminate over the wrongs we suffer at the hands of others and ignore the suffering we have inflicted on others. He that well and rightly considers his own works, will find little cause to judge harshly of another.

Daily Prayers to Recite: Litany of the Holy Ghost, Litany of the Blessed Virgin Mary, and Ave Maris Stella (see text of prayers at Appendix I)

Journal Entry:

Here are some sample questions to get you started:

- What feelings, reactions, intuitions, desires, emotions, thoughts, or insights did you encounter in prayer?
- What word, phrase, image, or memory meant most to you during prayer?
- Is there something happening in my life that is becoming part of my prayer?
- Do I feel moved to do something concrete in my life?

_____

_____

_____

_____

_____

_____

_____

_____

ST. LOUIS DE MONTFORT

DAY 17

Reading 1: *True Devotion To the Blessed Virgin Mary*, No. 228, "Preparatory Exercises" continued

Regarding judgment and the punishment of sinners, in all things look to the end. How will you stand before that strict Judge (Heb. 10:31) before whom nothing is hid? This Judge is not appeased with gifts and allows no excuses, but will judge according to right.

O wretched and foolish sinner! You, who can be terrified by the look of an angry man, what answer will you make to God who knows all your wickedness (Job 9:2)? Why do you not provide for yourself (Luke 16:9) for the day of judgment? On that day, no man can be excused or defended by another. On that day, every one must carry their own burdens.

Reading 2: Luke 16:1-8, "The Crafty Steward" or "The Parable of the Dishonest Manager"

Jesus also said to the disciples, "There was a rich man who had a steward, and charges were brought to him that this man was wasting his goods. And he called him and said to him, 'What is this that I hear about you? Turn in the account of your stewardship, for you can no longer be steward.' And the steward said to himself, 'What shall I do, since my master is taking the stewardship away from me? I am not strong enough to dig, and I am ashamed to beg. I have decided what to do, so that people may receive me into their houses when I am put out of the stewardship.'

So, summoning his master's debtors one by one, he said to the first, 'How much do you owe my master?' He said, 'A hundred measures of oil.' And he said to him, 'Take your bill, and sit down quickly and write fifty.' Then he said to another, 'And

77

how much do you owe?' He said, 'A hundred measures of wheat.' He said to him, 'Take your bill, and write eighty.' The master commended the dishonest steward for his prudence; for the sons of this world are wiser in their own generation than the sons of light.

Daily Prayers to Recite: Litany of the Holy Ghost, Litany of the Blessed Virgin Mary, and Ave Maris Stella (see text of prayers at Appendix I)

Journal Entry:

Here are some sample questions to get you started:

- What feelings, reactions, intuitions, desires, emotions, thoughts, or insights did you encounter in prayer?
- What word, phrase, image, or memory meant most to you during prayer?
- Is there something happening in my life that is becoming part of my prayer?
- Do I feel moved to do something concrete in my life?

_____

_____

_____

_____

_____

_____

_____

_____

_____

_____

_____

St. Louis de Montfort

DAY 18

Reading 1: Gospel of Luke 17:1-10

On Leading Others Astray
And he said to his disciples, "Temptations to sin are sure to come; but woe to him by whom they come! It would be better for him if a millstone were hung round his neck and he were cast into the sea, than that he should cause one of these little ones to sin."

On Brotherly Correction
"Take heed to yourselves; if your brother sins, rebuke him, and if he repents, forgive him; and if he sins against you seven times in the day, and turns to you seven times, and says, 'I repent,' you must forgive him."

The Power of Faith
The Apostles said to the Lord, "Increase our faith!" And the Lord said, "If you had faith as a grain of mustard seed, you could say to this mulberry tree, 'Be rooted up, and be planted in the sea,' and it would obey you."

Humble Service
"Will any one of you, who has a servant plowing or keeping sheep, say to him when he has come in from the field, 'Come at once and sit down at table'? Will he not rather say to him, 'Prepare supper for me, and gird yourself and serve me, till I eat and drink; and afterward you shall eat and drink'? Does he thank the servant because he did what was commanded? So you also, when you have done all that is commanded you, say, 'We are unworthy servants; we have only done what was our duty.'"

Reading 2: *Imitation of Christ* by Thomas á Kempis, Book III, Chapter 47, "That All Grievous Things are to be Suffered Joyfully for the Sake of Eternal Life"

My son, says the Lord, do not be wearied by the labors you have undertaken for My sake. Do not let tribulation cast you into despair. Instead, let My promise strengthen and comfort you in every circumstance. I am well able to reward you beyond all measure and imagination. You will not toil for long here, nor will you always be oppressed with grief. Await my promises, and you will see an end to all your trials.

Daily Prayers to Recite: Litany of the Holy Ghost, Litany of the Blessed Virgin Mary, and Ave Maris Stella (see text of prayers at Appendix I)

Journal Entry:

Here are some sample questions to get you started:

- What feelings, reactions, intuitions, desires, emotions, thoughts, or insights did you encounter in prayer?
- What word, phrase, image, or memory meant most to you during prayer?
- Is there something happening in my life that is becoming part of my prayer?
- Do I feel moved to do something concrete in my life?

_____

_____

_____

_____

_____

_____

_____

_____

DAY 19

Reading: Gospel of Luke 18:15-30

Jesus Blesses Little Children
Now they were bringing even infants to him that he might touch them; and when the disciples saw it, they rebuked them. But Jesus called them to him, saying, "Let the children come to me, and do not hinder them; for to such belongs the kingdom of God. Truly, I say to you, whoever does not receive the kingdom of God like a child shall not enter it."

The Rich Young Ruler
And a ruler asked him, "Good Teacher, what shall I do to inherit eternal life?" And Jesus said to him, "Why do you call me good? No one is good but God alone. You know the commandments: 'Do not commit adultery, Do not kill, Do not steal, Do not bear false witness, Honor your father and mother.'" And he said, "All these I have observed from my youth." And when Jesus heard it, he said to him, "One thing you still lack. Sell all that you have and distribute to the poor, and you will have treasure in heaven; and come, follow me." But when he heard this he became sad, for he was very rich.

The Danger of Riches
Jesus looking at him became sorrowful and said, "How hard it is for those who have riches to enter the kingdom of God! For it is easier for a camel to go through the eye of a needle than for a rich man to enter the kingdom of God." Those who heard it said, "Then who can be saved?" But he said, "What is impossible with men is possible with God."

The Reward of Renunciation
And Peter said, "Lo, we have left our homes and followed you." And he said to them, "Truly, I say to you, there is no man who has left house or wife or brothers or parents or children, for

the sake of the kingdom of God, who will not receive manifold more in this time, and in the age to come eternal life."

Daily Prayers to Recite: Daily Prayers to Recite: Litany of the Holy Ghost, Litany of the Blessed Virgin Mary, and Ave Maris Stella (see text of prayers at Appendix I)

Journal Entry:

Here are some sample questions to get you started:

- What feelings, reactions, intuitions, desires, emotions, thoughts, or insights did you encounter in prayer?
- What word, phrase, image, or memory meant most to you during prayer?
- Is there something happening in my life that is becoming part of my prayer?
- Do I feel moved to do something concrete in my life?

ST. LOUIS DE MONTFORT

SECOND WEEK

DAY 20

Theme for the Week: Knowledge of The Blessed Virgin

Acts of love, pious affection for the Blessed Virgin, imitation of her virtues, especially her profound humility, her lively faith, her blind obedience, her continual mental prayer, her mortification in all things, her surpassing purity, her ardent charity, her heroic patience, her angelic sweetness, and her divine wisdom: "there being," as St. Louis de Montfort says, "the ten principal virtues of the Blessed Virgin."

We must unite ourselves to Jesus through Mary. This is the principal characteristic of our devotion. Saint Louis de Montfort, therefore, asks that we employ ourselves in acquiring a knowledge of the Blessed Virgin.

Mary is our sovereign and our mediatrix, our Mother and our Mistress. Let us then endeavor to know the effects of this royalty, of this mediation, and of this maternity, as well as the grandeurs and prerogatives which are the foundation or consequences thereof. Our Mother is also a perfect mold wherein we are to be molded in order to make her intentions and dispositions ours. This we cannot achieve without studying the interior life of Mary. This means her virtues, her sentiments, her actions, her participation in the mysteries of Christ, and her union with Him.

Reading: Luke 2:16-21, 45-52

And they went with haste, and found Mary and Joseph, and the babe lying in a manger. And when they saw it they made known the saying which had been told them concerning this child; and all who heard it wondered at what the shepherds told them. But Mary kept all these things, pondering them in her heart. And the shepherds returned, glorifying and praising God for all they had heard and seen, as it had been told them.

And at the end of eight days, when he was circumcised, he was called Jesus, the name given by the angel before he was conceived in the womb.

[...] and when they did not find him, they returned to Jerusalem, seeking him. After three days they found him in the temple, sitting among the teachers, listening to them and asking them questions; and all who heard him were amazed at his understanding and his answers. And when they saw him they were astonished; and his mother said to him, "Son, why have you treated us so? Behold, your father and I have been looking for you anxiously." And he said to them, "How is it that you sought me? Did you not know that I must be in my Father's house?" And they did not understand the saying which he spoke to them. And he went down with them and came to Nazareth, and was obedient to them; and his mother kept all these things in her heart.

And Jesus increased in wisdom and in stature, and in favor with God and man.

Daily Prayers to Recite: Litany of the Holy Ghost, Litany of the Blessed Virgin Mary, Ave Maris Stella, St. Louis de Montfort's Prayer to Mary, and the Rosary (see text of prayers at Appendix I; see Appendix II for instructions on reciting the Rosary)

Journal Entry:

Here are some sample questions to get you started:

- What feelings, reactions, intuitions, desires, emotions, thoughts, or insights did you encounter in prayer?
- What word, phrase, image, or memory meant most to you during prayer?
- Is there something happening in my life that is becoming part of my prayer?
- Do I feel moved to do something concrete in my life?

_____

_____

_____

_____

_____

_____

_____

_____

_____

_____

_____

_____

_____

_____

_____

_____

_____

_____

_____

_____

St. Louis de Montfort

DAY 21

Reading: *True Devotion to the Blessed Virgin Mary*, Nos. 23-24

If we would go up to God and be united with Him, we must use *the same means* that He used to come down to us, to be made Man, and to impart His graces to us. This means is a true devotion to our Blessed Lady.

There are several true devotions to our Lady. I do not speak here of those which are false. The **first** consists in fulfilling our Christian duties, avoiding mortal sin, acting more out of love than fear, praying to our Lady now and then, and honoring her as the Mother of God – but without having any special devotion to her.

The **second** consists in fostering more perfect love for our Lady, as well as confidence and veneration. Such leads us to join the Confraternities of the Holy Rosary and of the Scapular, to recite the five or fifteen decades of the Holy Rosary, to honor Mary's images and altars, to publish her praises and to enroll ourselves in her modalities. This devotion is good, holy, and praiseworthy if we keep ourselves free from sin. But even this is not so perfect as the next. Nor is this way as efficient in severing our soul from creatures. That is, in detaching ourselves in order to be united with Jesus Christ.

The **third** devotion to our Lady, known and practiced by very few persons, is what I am about to disclose to you, whose soul is fixed on Heaven. It consists in giving one's self entirely and as a slave to Mary, and to Jesus through Mary, and after that, to do all that we do, through Mary, with Mary, in Mary, and for Mary.

We should choose a special feast day on which we give, consecrate, and sacrifice to Mary voluntarily, lovingly, and without constraint, entirely and without reserve the following:

- Our body and soul;
- Our families;
- Our exterior property, such as house and income; and
- Our interior and spiritual possessions, such as our merits, graces, virtues, and satisfactions.

Daily Prayers to Recite: Litany of the Holy Ghost, Litany of the Blessed Virgin Mary, Ave Maris Stella, St. Louis de Montfort's Prayer to Mary, and the Rosary (see text of prayers at Appendix I; see Appendix II for instructions on reciting the Rosary)

Journal Entry:

Here are some sample questions to get you started:

- What feelings, reactions, intuitions, desires, emotions, thoughts, or insights did you encounter in prayer?
- What word, phrase, image, or memory meant most to you during prayer?
- Is there something happening in my life that is becoming part of my prayer?
- Do I feel moved to do something concrete in my life?

ST. LOUIS DE MONTFORT

DAY 22

Reading: *True Devotion to the Blessed Virgin Mary*, Nos. 106-110, "Marks of authentic devotion to our Lady"

106. First, true devotion to our Lady is **interior**. It comes from within the mind and the heart and follows from the esteem in which we hold her, the high regard we have for her greatness, and the love we bear her.

107. Second, it is **trustful**. It fills us with confidence in the Blessed Virgin, the confidence that a child has for its loving Mother. It prompts us to go to her in every need of body and soul with great simplicity, trust, and affection.

108. Third, true devotion to our Lady is **holy**. It leads us to avoid sin and to imitate the virtues of Mary. Her ten principal virtues are deep humility, lively faith, blind obedience, unceasing prayer, constant self-denial, surpassing purity, ardent love, heroic patience, angelic kindness, and heavenly wisdom.

109. Fourth, true devotion to our Lady is **constant**. It strengthens us in our desire to do good and prevents us from giving up our devotional practices too easily. It gives us the courage to oppose the fashions and maxims of the world, the vexations and unruly inclinations of the flesh, and the temptations of the devil. Thus, a person truly devoted to our Blessed Lady is not changeable, fretful, scrupulous, or timid.

110. Fifth, true devotion to Mary is **disinterested**. It inspires us to seek God alone in his Blessed Mother and not ourselves. The true subject of Mary does not serve his illustrious Queen for selfish gain. He does not serve her for temporal or eternal

well-being, but simply and solely because she ought to be served and God alone in her.

Daily Prayers to Recite: Litany of the Holy Ghost, Litany of the Blessed Virgin Mary, Ave Maris Stella, St. Louis de Montfort's Prayer to Mary, and the Rosary (see text of prayers at Appendix I; see Appendix II for instructions on reciting the Rosary)

Journal Entry:

Here are some sample questions to get you started:

- What feelings, reactions, intuitions, desires, emotions, thoughts, or insights did you encounter in prayer?
- What word, phrase, image, or memory meant most to you during prayer?
- Is there something happening in my life that is becoming part of my prayer?
- Do I feel moved to do something concrete in my life?

_____

_____

_____

_____

_____

_____

_____

_____

_____

_____

_____

_____

ST. LOUIS DE MONTFORT

DAY 23

Reading: *True Devotion to the Blessed Virgin Mary*, Nos. 120-121, "Nature of perfect devotion to the Blessed Virgin or perfect consecration to Jesus Christ"

120. All perfection consists in our being conformed, united, and consecrated to Jesus. It naturally follows that the most perfect of all devotions is that which conforms, unites, and consecrates us most completely to Jesus. Of all God's creatures, Mary is the most conformed to Jesus.

Therefore, of all devotions, devotion to Mary makes for the most effective consecration and conformity to Jesus. The more one is consecrated to Mary, the more one is consecrated to Jesus. That is why perfect consecration to Jesus is a perfect and complete consecration of oneself to the Blessed Virgin. This is the devotion I teach. In other words, it is the perfect renewal of the vows and promises of Holy Baptism.

121. This devotion consists in giving oneself entirely to Mary in order to belong entirely to Jesus through her. It requires us to give the following:

(1) Our body with its senses and members;
(2) Our soul with its faculties;
(3) Our present material possessions and all we shall acquire in the future; and
(4) Our interior and spiritual possessions, that is, our merits, virtues, and good actions of the past, the present, and the future.

In other words, we give Mary all that we possess both in our natural life and in our spiritual life. Not only that, we give Mary everything we will acquire in the future in the order of nature, of grace, and of glory in heaven. This we do without the slightest reservation. We don't hold back even a penny, a hair, or the smallest good deed. And we give all this for all eternity without claiming or expecting anything in return for our offering and our service, except the honor of belonging to our Lord through Mary and in Mary. This we would do even if our Mother was not - as in fact she always is - the most generous and appreciative of all God's creatures.

Daily Prayers to Recite: Litany of the Holy Ghost, Litany of the Blessed Virgin Mary, Ave Maris Stella, St. Louis de Montfort's Prayer to Mary, and the Rosary (see text of prayers at Appendix I; see Appendix II for instructions on reciting the Rosary)

Journal Entry:

Here are some sample questions to get you started:

- What feelings, reactions, intuitions, desires, emotions, thoughts, or insights did you encounter in prayer?
- What word, phrase, image, or memory meant most to you during prayer?
- Is there something happening in my life that is becoming part of my prayer?
- Do I feel moved to do something concrete in my life?

_____

_____

_____

_____

_____

_____

_____

_____

_____

ST. LOUIS DE MONTFORT

DAY 24

Reading: *True Devotion to the Blessed Virgin Mary*, Nos. 152-164

This devotion is a smooth, short, perfect, and sure way of attaining union with our Lord Jesus, in which Christian perfection consists.

This devotion is a **smooth** way. It is the path which Jesus Christ, Himself, opened up in coming to us. Along this path, there is no obstruction to prevent us reaching him. It is quite true that we can attain to divine union by other roads, but these involve many more crosses, exceptional setbacks, and difficulties that we cannot easily overcome.

This devotion is a **short** way to discover Jesus. The road is short because we do not wander from it. The road is also short because, as we have just said, we walk along this road with greater ease and joy, and therefore with greater speed. We advance more in a brief period of submission to Mary and dependence on her than in whole years of self-will and self-reliance.

This devotion is a **perfect** way to reach our Lord and be united to him. This is because Mary is the most perfect and the most holy of all creatures, and because Jesus, who came to us in a perfect manner, chose no other road for his great and wonderful journey. The Most High, the Incomprehensible One, the Inaccessible One, He who is, deigned to come down to us poor earthly creatures who are nothing at all. How was this done? The Most High God came down to us in a perfect way through the humble Virgin Mary, without losing anything of his divinity or holiness. It is likewise through Mary that we poor creatures must ascend to almighty God in a perfect manner and without fear.

This devotion to our Lady is a **sure** way to go to Jesus and to acquire holiness through union with Him. The devotion which I teach is not new. Indeed, it could not be condemned without overthrowing the foundations of Christianity. It is obvious then that this devotion is not new. If it is not commonly practiced, it is because it is too sublime to be appreciated and undertaken by everyone. This devotion is a safe means of going to Jesus Christ, because it is Mary's role to lead us safely to her Son.

Daily Prayers to Recite: Litany of the Holy Ghost, Litany of the Blessed Virgin Mary, Ave Maris Stella, St. Louis de Montfort's Prayer to Mary, and the Rosary (see text of prayers at Appendix I; see Appendix II for instructions on reciting the Rosary)

Journal Entry:

Here are some sample questions to get you started:

- What feelings, reactions, intuitions, desires, emotions, thoughts, or insights did you encounter in prayer?
- What word, phrase, image, or memory meant most to you during prayer?
- Is there something happening in my life that is becoming part of my prayer?
- Do I feel moved to do something concrete in my life?

_____

_____

_____

_____

_____

_____

_____

ST. LOUIS DE MONTFORT

DAY 25

Reading: *True Devotion to the Blessed Virgin Mary*, Nos. 213-225, "Wonderful Effects of this Devotion"

My dear friend, be sure that if you remain faithful to the interior and exterior practices of this devotion, which I will point out, the following effects will be produced in your soul:

1. Knowledge of our unworthiness
By the light which the Holy Spirit will give you through Mary, his faithful spouse, you will perceive the evil inclinations of your fallen nature and how incapable you are of good. Finally, the humble Virgin Mary will share her humility with you so that, although you regard yourself with distaste and desire to be disregarded by others, you will not look down on anyone.

2. A share in Mary's faith
Mary will share her faith with you. Her faith on earth was stronger than that of all the patriarchs, prophets, apostles, and saints.

3. The gift of pure love
The Mother of fair love will rid your heart of all scruples and inordinate servile fear.

4. Great confidence in God and in Mary
Our Blessed Lady will fill you with unbounded confidence in God and in herself. This is because you will no longer approach Jesus by yourself but always through Mary, your loving Mother.

5. Communication of the spirit of Mary
The soul of Mary will be communicated to you to glorify the Lord. Her spirit will take the place of yours to rejoice in God,

her Savior, but only if you are faithful to the practices of this devotion.

6. Transformation into the likeness of Jesus
Mary, the Tree of Life, will be well cultivated in your soul by fidelity to this devotion. She will in due time bring forth her fruit, which is none other than Jesus.

7. The Greater Glory of Christ
If you live this devotion sincerely, you will give more glory to Jesus in a month than in many years of a more demanding devotion.

Daily Prayers to Recite: Litany of the Holy Ghost, Litany of the Blessed Virgin Mary, Ave Maris Stella, St. Louis de Montfort's Prayer to Mary, and the Rosary (see text of prayers at Appendix I; see Appendix II for instructions on reciting the Rosary)

Journal Entry:
Here are some sample questions to get you started:
- What feelings, reactions, intuitions, desires, emotions, thoughts, or insights did you encounter in prayer?
- What word, phrase, image, or memory meant most to you during prayer?
- Is there something happening in my life that is becoming part of my prayer?
- Do I feel moved to do something concrete in my life?

_____

_____

_____

_____

_____

_____

ST. LOUIS DE MONTFORT

DAY 26

Reading: *True Devotion to the Blessed Virgin Mary*, Nos. 12-38

"If you wish to understand the Mother," says a saint, "then understand the Son. She is a worthy Mother of God." Hic taceat omnis lingua: Here let every tongue be silent. My heart has dictated with special joy all that I have written to show that Mary has been unknown up till now, and that that is one of the reasons why Jesus Christ is not known as he should be. If then, as is certain, the knowledge and the kingdom of Jesus Christ must come into the world, it can only be as a necessary consequence of the knowledge and reign of Mary. She who first gave him to the world will establish his kingdom in the world.

With the whole Church I acknowledge that Mary, being a mere creature fashioned by the hands of God is, compared to his infinite majesty, less than an atom, or rather is simply nothing, since he alone can say, "I am he who is". Consequently, this great Lord, who is ever independent and self-sufficient, never had and does not now have any absolute need of the Blessed Virgin for the accomplishment of his will and the manifestation of his glory. To do all things he has only to will them. However, I declare that, considering things as they are, because God has decided to begin and accomplish his greatest works through the Blessed Virgin ever since he created her, we can safely believe that he will not change his plan in the time to come, for he is God and therefore does not change in his thoughts or his way of acting.

Mary is the Queen of heaven and earth by grace as Jesus is king by nature and by conquest. But as the kingdom of Jesus Christ exists primarily in the heart or interior of man, according to the words of the Gospel, "The kingdom of God is within you", so the kingdom of the Blessed Virgin is principally in the interior of man, that is, in his soul. It is principally in souls that she is glorified with her Son more than in any visible creature. So we may call her, as the saints do, Queen of our hearts.

Daily Prayers to Recite: Litany of the Holy Ghost, Litany of the Blessed Virgin Mary, Ave Maris Stella, St. Louis de Montfort's Prayer to Mary, and the Rosary (see text of prayers at Appendix I; see Appendix II for instructions on reciting the Rosary)

Journal Entry:

Here are some sample questions to get you started:

- What feelings, reactions, intuitions, desires, emotions, thoughts, or insights did you encounter in prayer?
- What word, phrase, image, or memory meant most to you during prayer?
- Is there something happening in my life that is becoming part of my prayer?
- Do I feel moved to do something concrete in my life?

_____

_____

_____

_____

_____

_____

_____

_____

_____

_____

St. Louis de Montfort

THIRD WEEK

DAY 27

Theme for the Week: Knowledge of Jesus Christ

During this period we will apply ourselves to the study of Jesus Christ. What is to be studied about Christ? First the God-Man, His grace and glory. Then, His rights to sovereign dominion over us; since, after having renounced Satan and the world, we have taken Jesus Christ for our Lord. The next object of our study is Jesus' exterior actions and His interior life. These include the virtues and acts of His Sacred Heart, His association with Mary in the mysteries of the Annunciation and Incarnation, His infancy and hidden life, the feast of Cana, and on Calvary.

Reading: *True Devotion to the Blessed Virgin Mary*, Nos. 61-62

61. Jesus, our Saviour, who is true God and true man, must be the ultimate end of all our devotions; otherwise they would be false and misleading. He is the Alpha and the Omega, the beginning and end of everything. "We labor," says St. Paul, "only to make all men perfect in Jesus Christ."

For in Jesus alone dwells the entire fullness of the divinity and the complete fullness of grace, virtue, and perfection. In Jesus alone, we have been blessed with every spiritual blessing. Jesus is the only teacher from whom we must learn. Jesus is the only Lord on whom we should depend. Jesus is the only

Head to whom we should be united, and the only model that we should imitate. Jesus is the only Physician that can heal us; the only Shepherd that can feed us; the only Way that can lead us; the only Truth that we can believe; the only Life that can animate us. Jesus alone is everything to us, and He alone can satisfy all our desires.

We are given no other name under heaven by which we can be saved. God has laid no other foundation for our salvation, perfection, and glory than Jesus. Every edifice which is not built on that firm rock, is founded upon shifting sands and will certainly fall sooner or later. Through him, with him, and in him, we can do all things and render all honor and glory to the Father in the unity of the Holy Spirit; we can make ourselves perfect; and we can be for our neighbor a fragrance of eternal life.

62. We are establishing sound devotion to our Blessed Mother *only* in order to establish devotion to our Lord more perfectly, by providing a smooth but certain way of reaching Jesus Christ. If devotion to our Lady distracts us from our Lord, we would have to reject it as an illusion of the devil. But this is far from being the case. As I have already shown and will show again later on, this devotion is necessary, simply and solely because it is a way of reaching Jesus perfectly, loving him tenderly, and serving him faithfully.

Daily Prayers to Recite: Litany of the Holy Ghost, Ave Maris Stella, Litany to the Holy Name, St. Louis de Montfort's Prayer to Mary, and O Jesus Living in Mary (see text of prayers at Appendix I)

Journal Entry:

Here are some sample questions to get you started:

- What feelings, reactions, intuitions, desires, emotions, thoughts, or insights did you encounter in prayer?
- What word, phrase, image, or memory meant most to you during prayer?
- Is there something happening in my life that is becoming part of my prayer?
- Do I feel moved to do something concrete in my life?

_____

_____

_____

_____

_____

_____

_____

_____

_____

_____

_____

_____

_____

_____

_____

_____

_____

_____

_____

_____

_____

_____

_____

_____

_____

_____

_____

_____

_____

_____

_____

_____

_____

_____

_____

_____

_____

_____

_____

_____

_____

_____

St. Louis de Montfort

DAY 28

Reading: Matthew 26:1-2, 26-29, 36-46

When Jesus had finished all these sayings, he said to his disciples: "You know that after two days the Passover is coming, and the Son of man will be delivered up to be crucified."

Now as they were eating, Jesus took bread, and blessed, and broke it, and gave it to the disciples and said, "Take, eat; this is my body." And he took a cup, and when he had given thanks he gave it to them, saying, "Drink of it, all of you; for this is my blood of the covenant, which is poured out for many for the forgiveness of sins. I tell you I shall not drink again of this fruit of the vine until that day when I drink it new with you in my Father's kingdom."

Then Jesus went with them to a place called Gethsemane, and he said to his disciples, "Sit here, while I go yonder and pray." And taking with him Peter and the two sons of Zebedee, he began to be sorrowful and troubled. Then he said to them, "My soul is very sorrowful, even to death; remain here, and watch with me." And going a little farther he fell on his face and prayed, "My Father, if it be possible, let this cup pass from me; nevertheless, not as I will, but as thou wilt." And he came to the disciples and found them sleeping; and he said to Peter, "So, could you not watch with me one hour? Watch and pray that you may not enter into temptation; the spirit indeed is willing, but the flesh is weak." Again, for the second time, he went away and prayed, "My Father, if this cannot pass unless I drink it, thy will be done." And again he came and found them sleeping, for their eyes were heavy. So, leaving them again, he went away and prayed for the third time, saying the same words. Then he came to the disciples and said to them, "Are you still sleeping and taking your rest? Behold, the hour is at hand, and the Son of man is betrayed into the hands of sinners. Rise, let us be going; see, my betrayer is at hand."

Daily Prayers to Recite: Litany of the Holy Ghost, Ave Maris Stella, Litany to the Holy Name, St. Louis de Montfort's Prayer to Mary, and O Jesus Living in Mary (see text of prayers at Appendix I)

Journal Entry:

Here are some sample questions to get you started:

- What feelings, reactions, intuitions, desires, emotions, thoughts, or insights did you encounter in prayer?
- What word, phrase, image, or memory meant most to you during prayer?
- Is there something happening in my life that is becoming part of my prayer?
- Do I feel moved to do something concrete in my life?

_____

_____

_____

_____

_____

_____

_____

_____

_____

_____

_____

_____

_____

ST. LOUIS DE MONTFORT

DAY 29

Reading: *Imitation of Christ* by Thomas á Kempis, Book I, Chapter 1, "Of the Imitation of Christ and Contempt for all the Vanities of the World"

He that follows Me, walks not in darkness (John 8:12), says the Lord. These words of Christ admonish us to imitate His life and manners to be truly enlightened and delivered from all blindness of heart.

Therefore, let our chief endeavor be to meditate upon the life of Jesus Christ. The teachings of Christ exceed all the words of the angels and saints. He whose soul beholds the Gospel will find therein the hidden manna (Revelation 2:17). But oftentimes, many who hear the Gospel of Christ, do not find such sweetness in them. This is because they do not have the Spirit of Christ. But whoever will fully understand the words of Christ, must conform his life wholly to the life of Christ.

What does it avail a man to speak profoundly of the Trinity, if he lacks of humility and thereby displeases the Trinity? Profound words do not make a man holy and just. It is a life of virtue which makes him dear to God. I would rather feel contrition for my sins, than merely know the definition of contrition. If you knew the whole Bible by heart and the writings of all the philosophers, what would it profit you without the love of God and His grace?

Vanity of vanities, all is vanity (Ecclesiastes 1:2), except to love God and to serve Him only. This is the highest wisdom: to draw daily nearer to God and the kingdom of heaven by despising the world.

Daily Prayers to Recite: Litany of the Holy Ghost, Ave Maris Stella, Litany to the Holy Name, St. Louis de Montfort's

Prayer to Mary, and O Jesus Living in Mary (see text of prayers at Appendix I)

Journal Entry:

Here are some sample questions to get you started:

- What feelings, reactions, intuitions, desires, emotions, thoughts, or insights did you encounter in prayer?
- What word, phrase, image, or memory meant most to you during prayer?
- Is there something happening in my life that is becoming part of my prayer?
- Do I feel moved to do something concrete in my life?

_____

_____

_____

_____

_____

_____

_____

_____

_____

_____

_____

_____

_____

_____

_____

_____

_____

ST. LOUIS DE MONTFORT

DAY 30

Reading 1: Matthew 27:36-44

Then [the soldiers] sat down and kept watch over him there. And over his head they put the charge against him, which read, "This is Jesus the King of the Jews." Then two robbers were crucified with him, one on the right and one on the left. And those who passed by derided him, wagging their heads and saying, "You who would destroy the temple and build it in three days, save yourself! If you are the Son of God, come down from the cross." So also the chief priests, with the scribes and elders, mocked him, saying, "He saved others; he cannot save himself. He is the King of Israel; let him come down now from the cross, and we will believe in him. He trusts in God; let God deliver him now, if he desires him; for he said, 'I am the Son of God.'" And the robbers who were crucified with him also reviled him in the same way.

Reading 2: *Imitation of Christ* by Thomas á Kempis, Book II, Chapter 12, "Of the King's High Way of the Holy Cross"

To many this seems a hard saying, "Deny yourself, take up your cross, and follow Me" (Matt. 16:24). But it will be much harder to hear this at the Last Judgment, "Depart from Me, you cursed, into everlasting fire" (Matt. 25:41). But they who now gladly hear and follow the words of Christ, need not fear hearing a sentence of eternal damnation. This sign of the Cross will appear in heaven when the Lord comes to judge the world (Matt. 24:30). Then all the servants of the Cross, who in their lifetime conformed themselves to Christ crucified, shall draw near to Christ the Judge with great confidence.

Why, then, do you fear to take up His Cross? It is the one and only way which leads to Heaven. In the Cross is salvation, in the Cross is life, in the Cross is protection against our enemies, in the Cross is the fullness of heavenly sweetness. In the Cross is strength of mind, in the Cross is joy of spirit, in the Cross is the height of virtue, in the Cross is the perfection of holiness.

Take up, therefore, your Cross and follow Jesus into life everlasting.

Daily Prayers to Recite: Litany of the Holy Ghost, Ave Maris Stella, Litany to the Holy Name, St. Louis de Montfort's Prayer to Mary, and O Jesus Living in Mary (see text of prayers at Appendix I)

Journal Entry:

Here are some sample questions to get you started:
- What feelings, reactions, intuitions, desires, emotions, thoughts, or insights did you encounter in prayer?
- What word, phrase, image, or memory meant most to you during prayer?
- Is there something happening in my life that is becoming part of my prayer?
- Do I feel moved to do something concrete in my life?

_____

_____

_____

_____

_____

_____

_____

_____

_____

_____

ST. LOUIS DE MONTFORT

DAY 31

Reading 1: *Imitation of Christ* by Thomas á Kempis, Book IV, Chapter 2, "That the Great Goodness of God is Given to Man in the Blessed Sacrament"

My Lord Jesus, confident of your goodness and great mercy, I draw near. I come to You as a sick man comes to the Healer, as a hungry and thirsty man comes to the Fountain of life, as a needy man to the King of Heaven. I come as a servant to the Lord, a creature to the Creator, and as afflicted to the Comforter.

"But how is it that You come to me? Who am I that You give Yourself to me? How dare I, a sinner, appear before You? And how is it that You would come to such a sinner? You know me and are well aware that I have nothing to repay You with for such grace. I confess, therefore, my own unworthiness and acknowledge Your goodness. I praise Your tender mercy and give thanks for your infinite charity.

Reading 2: *True Devotion to the Blessed Virgin Mary*, Nos. 243-254

Loving slaves of Jesus in Mary should hold in high esteem the devotion to Jesus, the Word of God, in the great mystery of the Incarnation, March 25th (Feast of the Annunciation). This is the mystery proper to this devotion, because it was inspired by the Holy Spirit for the following reasons:

- That we might honor and imitate the wondrous dependence which God the Son chose to have on Mary, for the glory of His Father and for the redemption of man. This dependence is revealed especially in this mystery where Jesus becomes a captive and slave in the womb of his Blessed Mother, depending on her for everything.

- That we might thank God for the incomparable graces he has conferred upon Mary, especially that of choosing her to be his most worthy Mother. This choice was made in the mystery of the Incarnation. These are the two principal ends of the slavery of Jesus in Mary.

We live in an age of pride when a great number of haughty scholars find fault even with long-established and sound devotions. Because of these, it is better to speak of "slavery of Jesus in Mary" and to call oneself "slave of Jesus" rather than "slave of Mary". We then avoid giving any pretext for criticism. In this way, we name this devotion after its ultimate end which is Jesus, rather than after the way and the means to arrive there, which is Mary. However, we can very well use either term without any scruple, as I myself do.

The principal mystery celebrated and honored in this devotion is the mystery of the Incarnation when we find Jesus only in Mary, having become incarnate in her womb. Therefore, it is appropriate for us to say, "slavery of Jesus in Mary," and of Jesus dwelling enthroned in Mary, "O Jesus living in Mary," according to the beautiful prayer recited by so many great souls.

Those who accept this devotion should have a great love for the "Hail Mary", or, as it is also called, the "Angelic Salutation". Few Christians, however enlightened they may be, understand the value, merit, excellence, and necessity of the Hail Mary. Our Blessed Lady herself had to appear on several occasions to men of great holiness and insight, such as St. Dominic, St. John Capistrano, and Blessed Alan de Rupe, to convince them of the richness of this prayer.

Daily Prayers to Recite: Litany of the Holy Ghost, Ave Maris Stella, Litany to the Holy Name, St. Louis de Montfort's

Prayer to Mary, and O Jesus Living in Mary (see text of prayers at Appendix I)

Journal Entry:

Here are some sample questions to get you started:

- What feelings, reactions, intuitions, desires, emotions, thoughts, or insights did you encounter in prayer?
- What word, phrase, image, or memory meant most to you during prayer?
- Is there something happening in my life that is becoming part of my prayer?
- Do I feel moved to do something concrete in my life?

_____

_____

_____

_____

_____

_____

_____

_____

_____

_____

_____

_____

_____

_____

_____

ST. LOUIS DE MONTFORT

DAY 32

Reading 1: *Imitation of Christ* by Thomas á Kempis, Book II, Chapter 7, "Of the Love of Jesus above All Things"

Blessed is he who knows how good it is to love Jesus and to despise himself for Jesus' sake. A man ought to forsake what he loves for the sake of the Beloved, because Jesus must be loved above all things (Deut. 6:5; Matt. 22:37).

The love of created things is deceitful and disappointing, while the love of Jesus is faithful and persevering. He who clings to a creature will fall as that creature falls, while he who embraces Jesus will be made strong forever.

Love Jesus and hold onto Him as your friend. When all others forsake you, He will not. Nor will Jesus allow you to perish in the end. At some point whether you choose to or not, you will be separated from all men. Therefore, both in life and death, keep yourself close to Jesus. Commit yourself to faithfulness to Him, Who remains and will help you even when all else fail.

Your Beloved is of such a nature, that He will allow no rival. Jesus alone will have your heart, which is His throne, and He will rule there as King. If you could empty yourself completely of the love of creatures, Jesus would dwell with you and never forsake you.

Reading 2: *True Devotion to the Blessed Virgin Mary*, Nos. 61-62

There are some interior practices which are very sanctifying for those souls which the Holy Spirit calls to a high degree of perfection. They may be expressed in four words: doing everything *through* Mary, *with* Mary, *in* Mary, and *for* Mary.

We do these that we may do it more perfectly *through* Jesus, *with* Jesus, *in* Jesus, and *for* Jesus.

Through Mary
We must do everything through Mary. That is, we must obey her always and be led in all things by her spirit, which is the Holy Spirit of God. "Those who are led by the Spirit of God are children of God," says St. Paul. Those who are led by the spirit of Mary are children of Mary, and, therefore, children of God.

Among the many servants of Mary only those who are truly and faithfully devoted to her are led by her spirit. I have said that the spirit of Mary is the Spirit of God because she was never led by her own spirit, but always by the Holy Spirit. The Holy Spirit made Himself master of her to such an extent that He became her very spirit. That is why St. Ambrose says, "May the soul of Mary be in each one of us to glorify the Lord. May the spirit of Mary be in each one of us to rejoice in God."

Happy is the man who follows the example of the good Jesuit Brother Rodriguez. Rodriguez died a holy death, because he was completely possessed and governed by the spirit of Mary, a spirit which is gentle yet strong, zealous yet prudent, humble yet courageous, pure yet fruitful.

With Mary
We must do everything with Mary. That is to say, we must look upon Mary in all our actions. Although she was a simple human being, she is the perfect model of every virtue and perfection. She was fashioned by the Holy Spirit for us to imitate, as far as our limited capacity allows.

In every action, we should consider how Mary performed it or how she would perform it if she were in our place. For this reason, we must examine and meditate on the great virtues she practiced during her life, especially:

1. Her lively faith, by which she believed the angel's word without the least hesitation, and believed faithfully and constantly even to the foot of the Cross on Calvary; and
2. Her deep humility, which made her prefer seclusion, maintain silence, submit to every eventuality, and put herself in the last place.

Daily Prayers to Recite: Litany of the Holy Ghost, Ave Maris Stella, Litany to the Holy Name, St. Louis de Montfort's Prayer to Mary, and O Jesus Living in Mary (see text of prayers at Appendix I)

Journal Entry:

Here are some sample questions to get you started:

- What feelings, reactions, intuitions, desires, emotions, thoughts, or insights did you encounter in prayer?
- What word, phrase, image, or memory meant most to you during prayer?
- Is there something happening in my life that is becoming part of my prayer?
- Do I feel moved to do something concrete in my life?

_____

_____

_____

_____

_____

_____

_____

_____

_____

St. Louis de Montfort

DAY 33

Reading 1: *Imitation of Christ* by Thomas á Kempis, Book IV, Chapter 11, "That the Body and Blood of Christ and Holy Scripture are Most Necessary for the Health of a Man's Soul"

Lord Jesus, how sweet it is to the devout soul to feast with You in Your banquet, where there is no other food but Yourself, which is the only Beloved of the devout soul and most desired in his heart! To me, it would also be sweet to pour forth tears in Your Presence from the very bottom of my heart. Sweeter still, would it be to wash Your feet with my tears alongside the blessed woman, Mary Magdalene (Luke 7:38).

But where is that devotion? Where is that bountiful flowing of holy tears? Surely in the sight of You and Your holy Angels, my whole heart ought to burn and to weep for joy. For in this Sacrament, You are mystically present and hidden under another shape.

And why? My eyes would not be able to endure looking upon You in Your Divine brightness. Neither could even the whole world stand in the glorious splendor of Your majesty. In this, You have regard for my weakness, that You would hide Yourself under this Sacrament.

Reading 2: *True Devotion to the Blessed Virgin Mary*, Nos. 261-65

As we discussed yesterday, there are some interior practices which are very sanctifying. They may be expressed in four words: doing everything *through* Mary, *with* Mary, *in* Mary, and *for* Mary. We discussed *through* and *with* Mary yesterday, and will turn now to *in* and *for* Mary. Remember, we do these that we may do it more perfectly *through* Jesus, *with* Jesus, *in* Jesus, and *for* Jesus.

In Mary

We must do everything in Mary. To understand this, we must realize that the Blessed Virgin is the true **Eden**. She is the earthly paradise of the new Adam, and the ancient paradise was only a symbol pointing toward her. There are in this earthly paradise untold riches, beauties, rarities, and delights. These were all left there by the new Adam, Jesus Christ. It is in this paradise that for nine months He "took his delights", worked his wonders, and displayed his riches with the magnificence of God, Himself.

The real **Tree of Life** grows in this earthly paradise. This is the Tree of Life which bore our Lord, who is the Fruit of Life. This is also the real Tree of Knowledge of Good and Evil, which bore the Light of the world. In this divine place, there are trees planted by the hand of God and watered by His divine unction. These trees have borne and continue to bear fruit that is pleasing to Him.

Only the Holy Spirit can teach us the truths that these material objects symbolize. The Holy Spirit, speaking through the Fathers of the Church, calls Our Lady the **Eastern Gate**. It is through the Eastern Gate that the High Priest, Jesus Christ, enters and goes out into the world. Through this gate He entered the world the first time, and through this same gate He will come the second time.

For Mary

Finally, we must do everything for Mary. We take Mary for our proximate, not ultimate, end. She is our mysterious intermediary and the easiest way of reaching Him. Relying on her protection, we should undertake and carry out great things for our noble Queen. We must defend her privileges when they are questioned and uphold her good name when it is under attack. We must attract everyone, if possible, to her service and to this true and sound devotion. As a reward for these little services, we should expect nothing in return, save the honor of belonging to such a lovable Queen and the joy of being united through her to Jesus, her Son, by a bond that is indissoluble in time and in eternity.

Daily Prayers to Recite: Litany of the Holy Ghost, Ave Maris Stella, Litany to the Holy Name, St. Louis de Montfort's Prayer to Mary, and O Jesus Living in Mary (see text of prayers at Appendix I)

Journal Entry:

Here are some sample questions to get you started:

- What feelings, reactions, intuitions, desires, emotions, thoughts, or insights did you encounter in prayer?
- What word, phrase, image, or memory meant most to you during prayer?
- Is there something happening in my life that is becoming part of my prayer?
- Do I feel moved to do something concrete in my life?

_____

_____

_____

_____

_____

_____

_____

_____

_____

_____

_____

_____

ST. LOUIS DE MONTFORT

DAY 34: DAY OF CONSECRATION

On the Day of Consecration, either fast, give alms, or offer a votive candle for the good of another (or all of the above). Do some spiritual penance and approach consecration in the spirit of mortification.

Now, go to Confession. If it is not possible to go to Confession on the Day of Consecration, go during the eight days prior.

Having gone to Confession, next receive Communion with the intention of giving yourself to Jesus, as a slave of love, by the hands of Mary. Try to receive Communion according to the method described in the Supplement of the book, "True Devotion to the Blessed Virgin Mary." See "Method of Communion" supplement below.

Now, pray the words of the consecration. Bring a copy of this consecration, such as the one provided in *The Catholic ManBook*, with you to church. Read it after Mass, either in front of the tabernacle or before the exposed Blessed Sacrament would be ideal. Sign your copy of the Act of Consecration.

Here are the words of consecration:

> O, Eternal and Incarnate Wisdom! O sweetest and most adorable Jesus! True God and true man, only Son of the Eternal Father, and of Mary, always virgin! I adore You profoundly in the bosom and splendors of Your Father during eternity, and I adore You also in the virginal bosom of Mary, Your most worthy Mother, in the time of Your incarnation.
>
> I give You thanks that You have annihilated Yourself, taking the form of a slave in order to rescue me from

the cruel slavery of the devil. I praise and glorify You for You have been pleased to submit Yourself to Mary, Your holy Mother, in all things, in order to make me Your faithful slave through her.

But, alas! Ungrateful and faithless as I have been, I have not kept the promises which I made so solemnly to You in my Baptism. I have not fulfilled my obligations. I do not deserve to be called Your child, nor even Your slave. As there is nothing in me which does not merit Your anger and repulse, I dare not come by myself before You, most holy and august Majesty. It is on this account that I have recourse to the intercession of Your most holy Mother, whom You have given me for a mediatrix with You. It is through her that I hope to obtain from You the following: contrition, the pardon of my sins, and the acquisition and preservation of wisdom.

Hail, then, O Immaculate Mary, living tabernacle of the Divinity, where the Eternal Wisdom willed to be hidden and to be adored by angels and by men! Hail, O Queen of Heaven and earth, to whose empire everything is subject which is under God. Hail, O sure refuge of sinners, whose mercy fails no one. Hear the desires which I have of the Divine Wisdom. For that end, receive the vows and offerings which I present to you in my lowliness.

I, _____ [your name], a faithless sinner, renew and ratify today in your hands the vows of my Baptism. I renounce forever Satan, his pomps and works. I give myself entirely to Jesus Christ, the Incarnate Wisdom, to carry my cross after Him all the days of my life, and to be more faithful to Him than I have ever been before. In the presence of all the heavenly court, I choose you this day for my Mother and Mistress. I deliver and consecrate to you, as your slave, my body and soul, my goods, both interior and exterior, and even the value of all my good actions, past, present, and future. I leave to you the entire and full right of disposing of me and all that belongs to me, without exception, according to your good pleasure, for the greater glory of God in time and in eternity.

Receive, O kindest Virgin, this little offering of my slavery, in honor of, and in union with, that subjection which the Eternal Wisdom deigned to have to your maternity. Receive this little offering in homage to the power which both of you have over this poor sinner. Receive this little offering also in thanksgiving for the privileges with which the Holy Trinity has favored you. I declare that I wish henceforth, as your true slave, to seek your honor and to obey you in all things.

O admirable Mother, present me to your dear Son as His eternal slave. As He has redeemed me by you, by you may He receive me! O Mother of mercy, grant me the grace to obtain the true Wisdom of God. For that end, receive me among those whom you love and teach, whom you lead, nourish, and protect as your children and your slaves.

O faithful Virgin, make me in all things so perfect a disciple, imitator, and slave of the Incarnate Wisdom, Jesus Christ thy Son, that I may attain, by your intercession and by your example, to the fullness of His age on earth and of His glory in Heaven. Amen.

_____

Sign your name here

_____

Date

Journal Entry:

Here are some sample questions to get you started:

- What feelings, reactions, intuitions, desires, emotions, thoughts, or insights did you encounter in prayer?
- What word, phrase, image, or memory meant most to you during prayer?
- Is there something happening in my life that is becoming part of my prayer?
- Do I feel moved to do something concrete in my life?

_____

_____

_____

_____

_____

_____

_____

_____

_____

_____

_____

_____

_____

_____

_____

_____

ST. LOUIS DE MONTFORT

After Consecration

Once you have consecrated yourself to Jesus through Mary, *live* that consecration. St. Louis-Marie de Montfort, the author of this Marian consecration, recommended the following:

- Keep praying to develop a "great contempt" for the spirit of this world and material things.
- Maintain a special devotion to the Mystery of the Incarnation. This can be done through meditation, spiritual reading, or by focusing on the feasts centering around the Incarnation, such as the Annunciation and the Nativity.
- Frequently recite the Hail Mary, Rosary, and the Magnificat. You may have discovered new Marian prayers during this consecration, such as the "Ave Maris Stella" or one of the litanies, that you may want to begin reciting, as well.
- Recite, every day if it is not inconvenient, the "Little Crown of the Blessed Virgin". This is a series of Our Fathers, Hail Marys, and Glory Bes, one Hail Mary for each of the twelve stars in the Virgin's Crown. St. Louis has a special way of praying the Little Crown, which is recommended.
- Do everything through, with, in, and for Mary for the sake of Jesus, with the prayer, "I am all thine Immaculate One, with all that I have in time and in eternity" in your heart and on your lips.
- Associate yourself with Mary in a special way before, during, and after Communion. See "Method of Communion" supplement below.
- Wear a little iron chain, such as around the neck, arm, waist, or ankle, as an outward sign and reminder of your holy slavery. This practice is optional, but very

recommended by St. Louis, though he does not further specify the appearance of such a chain.

- Renew the consecration once a year on the same date as signed above or another Feast day of your choosing, and by following the same 33-day period of exercises. If desired, also renew the consecration monthly with the prayer, "I am all yours and all I have is yours, O dear Jesus, through Mary, Your holy Mother."
- Join a Confraternity of Mary, such the Confraternity of Mary, Queen of All Hearts.

SUPPLEMENT: THIS DEVOTION AT HOLY COMMUNION

[From *True Devotion to Mary*, Nos. 266-273]

Before Holy Communion

1. Place yourself humbly in the presence of God.
2. Renounce your corrupt nature and dispositions, no matter how good self-love makes them appear to you.
3. Renew your consecration saying, "I belong entirely to you, dear Mother, and all that I have is yours."
4. Implore Mary to lend you her heart so that you may receive her Son with her dispositions. Remind her that her Son's glory requires that He should not come into a heart so sullied and fickle as your own, which could not fail to diminish His glory and might cause Him to leave. Tell her that if she will take up her home in you to receive her Son - which she can do because of her sovereignty over all hearts - He will be received by her in a perfect manner without danger of being affronted or being forced to depart. "God is in the midst of her. She shall not be moved."
5. Tell her with confidence that all you have given her of your possessions is little enough to honor her, but that in Holy Communion you wish to give her the same gifts as the eternal Father gave her. She will feel more honored than if you gave her all the wealth in the world.

6. Tell her, finally, that Jesus, whose love for her is unique, still wishes to take His delight and His repose in her even in your soul. And this, even though your soul is poorer and less clean than the stable which He readily entered, because she was there. Beg her to lend you her heart, saying, "O Mary, I take you for my all. Give me your heart."

During Holy Communion

After the Our Father, when you are about to receive our Lord, say to Him three times the prayer, "Lord, I am not worthy," as you would say it to each member of the Trinity:

1. Say it the first time as if you were telling the eternal Father that because of your evil thoughts and your ingratitude to such a good Father, you are unworthy to receive his only-begotten Son. But here is Mary, His handmaid, who acts for you and whose presence gives you a special confidence and hope in Him.

2. Say to God the Son, "Lord, I am not worthy." Say it meaning that you are not worthy to receive Him because of your useless and evil words and your carelessness in His service. Nevertheless, you ask Him to have pity on you because you are going to usher Him into the house of His Mother and yours, and you will not let Him go until He has made it His home. Implore Him to rise and come to the place of His repose and the ark of His sanctification. Tell Him that you have no faith in your own merits, strength, and preparedness, like Esau, but only in Mary, your Mother, just as Jacob had trust in Rebecca his mother. Tell Him that although you are a great sinner, you still presume to approach Him, supported by His holy Mother and adorned with her merits and virtues.

3. Say to the Holy Spirit, "Lord, I am not worthy". Tell Him that you are not worthy to receive the masterpiece of His love because of your lukewarmness, wickedness, and resistance to His inspirations. But, nonetheless, you put all your confidence in Mary, His faithful Spouse, and say with St. Bernard, "She is my greatest safeguard, the whole foundation of my hope." Beg Him to overshadow Mary, His inseparable Spouse, once again. Her womb is as pure and her heart as ardent as ever. Tell Him that if He does not enter your soul neither Jesus nor Mary will be formed there, nor will it be a worthy dwelling for them.

After Holy Communion

After Holy Communion, close your eyes and recollect yourself. Then usher Jesus into the heart of Mary. You are giving Him to His Mother. She will receive Him with great love, give Him the place of honor, adore Him profoundly, show Him perfect love, embrace Him intimately in spirit and in truth, and perform many offices for Him of which we, in our ignorance, would know nothing.

Or, maintain a profoundly humble heart in the presence of Jesus dwelling in Mary. Be in attendance like a slave at the gate of the royal palace, where the King is speaking with the Queen. While they are talking to each other, with no need of you, go in spirit to heaven and to the whole world. Call then upon all creatures to thank, adore, and love Jesus and Mary for you. "Come, let us adore."

Or, ask Jesus living in Mary that His kingdom may come upon earth through His holy Mother. Ask for divine wisdom, divine love, the forgiveness of your sins, or any other grace, but always through Mary and in Mary. Cast a look of reproach upon yourself and say, "Lord, do not look at my sins, let Your eyes see nothing in me, but the virtues and merits of Mary."

Remembering your sins, you may add, "I am my own worst enemy, and I am guilty of all these sins." Or, "Deliver me from the unjust and deceitful man that I am." Or again, "Dear Jesus, you must increase in my soul and I must decrease." "Mary, you must increase in me and I must always go on decreasing." "O Jesus and Mary, increase in me and increase in others around me."

There are innumerable other thoughts with which the Holy Spirit will inspire you, which He will make yours if you are thoroughly recollected and mortified, and constantly faithful to the great and sublime devotion which I have been teaching you.

But remember, the more you let Mary act in your communion, the more Jesus will be glorified. The more you humble yourself and listen to Jesus and Mary in peace and silence - with no desire to see, taste, or feel - the more freedom you will give to Mary to act in Jesus' name and the more Jesus will act in Mary. For the just man lives everywhere by faith, but especially in Holy Communion, which is an act of faith.

Appendix I: Prayers Recited during the Consecration

VENI CREATOR

Come, Holy Spirit, Creator blest,
and in our souls take up Thy rest;
come with Thy grace and heavenly aid
to fill the hearts which Thou hast made.

O comforter, to Thee we cry,
O heavenly gift of God Most High,
O fount of life and fire of love,
and sweet anointing from above.

Thou in Thy sevenfold gifts are known;
Thou, finger of God's hand we own;
Thou, promise of the Father,
Thou Who dost the tongue with power imbue.

Kindle our sense from above,
and make our hearts o'erflow with love;
with patience firm and virtue high
the weakness of our flesh supply.

Far from us drive the foe we dread,
and grant us Thy peace instead;
so shall we not, with Thee for guide,
turn from the path of life aside.

Oh, may Thy grace on us bestow
the Father and the Son to know;
and Thee, through endless times confessed,
of both the eternal Spirit blest.

Now to the Father and the Son,
Who rose from death, be glory given,
with Thou, O Holy Comforter,
henceforth by all in earth and heaven. Amen.

AVE MARIS STELLA

Hail, O Star of the ocean,
God's own Mother blest,
ever sinless Virgin,
gate of heav'nly rest.

Taking that sweet Ave,
which from Gabriel came,
peace confirm within us,
changing Eve's name.

Break the sinners' fetters,
make our blindness day,
Chase all evils from us,
for all blessings pray.

Show thyself a Mother,
may the Word divine
born for us thine Infant
hear our prayers through thine.

Virgin all excelling,
mildest of the mild,
free from guilt preserve us
meek and undefiled.

Keep our life all spotless,
make our way secure
till we find in Jesus,
joy for evermore.

Praise to God the Father,
honor to the Son,
in the Holy Spirit,
be the glory one. Amen

MAGNIFICAT

(Lk 1:46-55)

My soul proclaims the greatness of the Lord,
my spirit rejoices in God my Savior
for he has looked with favor on his lowly servant.
From this day all generations will call me blessed:
the Almighty has done great things for me,
and holy is his Name.

He has mercy on those who fear him
in every generation.
He has shown the strength of his arm,
he has scattered the proud in their conceit.

He has cast down the mighty from their thrones,
and has lifted up the lowly.
He has filled the hungry with good things,
and the rich he has sent away empty.

He has come to the help of his servant Israel
for he remembered his promise of mercy,
the promise he made to our fathers,
to Abraham and his children forever. Amen.

GLORY BE

Glory be to the Father,
and to the Son,
and to the Holy Ghost.
As it was in the beginning,
is now,
and ever shall be,
world without end. Amen.

LITANY OF THE HOLY GHOST

Lord, *have mercy on us.*
Christ, *have mercy on us.*
Lord, *have mercy on us.*

Father all powerful, *have mercy on us*
Jesus, Eternal Son of the Father, Redeemer of the world, *save us.*
Spirit of the Father and the Son, boundless life of both, *sanctify us.*
Holy Trinity, *hear us.*

Holy Ghost, Who proceeds from the Father and the Son, *enter our hearts.*
Holy Ghost, Who are equal to the Father and the Son, *enter our hearts.*

Promise of God the Father, *have mercy on us.*
Ray of heavenly light, *have mercy on us.*
Author of all good, *have mercy on us.*
Source of heavenly water, *have mercy on us.*
Consuming fire, *have mercy on us.*
Ardent charity, *have mercy on us.*
Spiritual unction, *have mercy on us.*
Spirit of love and truth, *have mercy on us.*
Spirit of wisdom and understanding, *have mercy on us.*
Spirit of counsel and fortitude, *have mercy on us.*
Spirit of knowledge and piety, *have mercy on us.*
Spirit of the fear of the Lord, *have mercy on us.*
Spirit of grace and prayer, *have mercy on us.*
Spirit of peace and meekness, *have mercy on us.*
Spirit of modesty and innocence, *have mercy on us.*
Holy Ghost, the Comforter, *have mercy on us.*
Holy Ghost, the Sanctifier, *have mercy on us.*
Holy Ghost, Who governs the Church, *have mercy on us.*
Gift of God, the Most High, *have mercy on us.*

Spirit Who fills the universe, *have mercy on us.*
Spirit of the adoption of the children of God, *have mercy on us.*

Holy Ghost, inspire us with horror of sin.
Holy Ghost, come and renew the face of the earth.
Holy Ghost, shed Thy light in our souls.
Holy Ghost, engrave Thy law in our hearts
Holy Ghost, inflame us with the flame of Thy love.
Holy Ghost, open to us the treasures of Thy graces
Holy Ghost, teach us to pray well.
Holy Ghost, enlighten us with Thy heavenly inspirations.
Holy Ghost, lead us in the way of salvation
Holy Ghost, grant us the only necessary knowledge.
Holy Ghost, inspire in us the practice of good.
Holy Ghost, grant us the merits of all virtues.
Holy Ghost, make us persevere in justice.
Holy Ghost, be Thou our everlasting reward.

Lamb of God, Who takes away the sins of the world, Send us Thy Holy Ghost.
Lamb of God, Who takes away the sins of the world, pour down into our souls the gifts of the Holy Ghost.
Lamb of God, Who takes away the sins of the world, grant us the Spirit of wisdom and piety.

V. Come, Holy Ghost! Fill the hearts of Thy faithful,
R. And enkindle in them the fire of Thy love.

Let Us Pray:
Grant, o merciful Father, that Your Divine Spirit may enlighten, inflame and purify us, that He may penetrate us with His heavenly dew and make us fruitful in good works, through Our Lord Jesus Christ, Your Son, Who with You, in the unity of the same Spirit, lives and reigns forever and ever. Amen.

Litany of the Blessed Virgin Mary (Litany of Loreto)

Lord, *have mercy on us.*
Christ, *have mercy on us.*

Lord, *have mercy on us.*
Christ hear us. *Christ, graciously hear us.*

God, the Father of heaven, *Have mercy on us.*
God, the Son, Redeemer of the world, *Have mercy on us.*
God, the Holy Ghost, *Have mercy on us.*
Holy Trinity, One God, *Have mercy on us.*

Holy Mary, *pray for us.*
Holy Mother of God, *pray for us.*
Holy Virgin of virgins, *pray for us.*
Mother of Christ, *pray for us.*
Mother of divine grace, *pray for us.*
Mother most pure, *pray for us.*
Mother most chaste, *pray for us.*
Mother inviolate, *pray for us.*
Mother undefiled, *pray for us.*
Mother most amiable, *pray for us.*
Mother most admirable, *pray for us.*
Mother of good counsel, *pray for us.*
Mother of our Creator, *pray for us.*
Mother of our Savior, *pray for us.*
Virgin most prudent, *pray for us.*
Virgin most venerable, *pray for us.*
Virgin most renowned, *pray for us.*
Virgin most powerful, *pray for us.*
Virgin most merciful, *pray for us.*
Virgin most faithful, *pray for us.*
Mirror of justice, *pray for us.*

Seat of wisdom, *pray for us.*
Cause of our joy, *pray for us.*
Spiritual vessel, *pray for us.*
Vessel of honor, *pray for us.*
Singular vessel of devotion, *pray for us.*
Mystical rose, *pray for us.*
Tower of David, *pray for us.*
Tower of ivory, *pray for us.*
House of gold, *pray for us.*
Ark of the covenant, *pray for us.*
Gate of Heaven, *pray for us.*
Morning star, *pray for us.*
Health of the sick, *pray for us.*
Refuge of sinners, *pray for us.*
Comforter of the afflicted, *pray for us.*
Help of Christians, *pray for us.*
Queen of angels, *pray for us.*
Queen of patriarchs, *pray for us.*
Queen of prophets, *pray for us.*
Queen of apostles, *pray for us.*
Queen of martyrs, *pray for us.*
Queen of confessors, *pray for us.*
Queen of virgins, *pray for us.*
Queen of all saints, *pray for us.*
Queen conceived without original sin, *pray for us.*
Queen assumed into heaven, *pray for us.*
Queen of the most holy Rosary, *pray for us.*
Queen of peace, *pray for us.*

Lamb of God, who takest away the sins of the world, *Spare us, O Lord.*
Lamb of God, who takest away the sins of the world, *Graciously hear us O Lord.*
Lamb of God, who takest away the sins of the world, *Have mercy on us.*

V. Pray for us, O holy Mother of God.
R. That we may be made worthy of the promises of Christ.

Let us pray:
Grant, O Lord God, we beseech Thee, that we Thy servants may rejoice in continual health of mind and body; and, through the glorious intercession of Blessed Mary ever Virgin, may be freed from present sorrow, and enjoy eternal gladness. Through Christ our Lord. Amen.

LITANY OF THE HOLY NAME OF JESUS

Lord, *have mercy on us.*
Christ, *have mercy on us.*

Lord, *have mercy on us.*
Christ hear us. *Christ, graciously hear us.*

God, the Father of heaven, *Have mercy on us.*
God, the Son, Redeemer of the world, *Have mercy on us.*
God, the Holy Ghost, *Have mercy on us.*
Holy Trinity, One God, *Have mercy on us.*

Jesus, Son of the living God, *have mercy on us.*
Jesus, splendor of the Father, *have mercy on us.*
Jesus, brightness of eternal light, *have mercy on us.*
Jesus, King of glory, *have mercy on us.*
Jesus, sun of justice, *have mercy on us.*
Jesus, Son of the Virgin Mary, *have mercy on us.*
Jesus, most amiable, *have mercy on us.*
Jesus, most admirable, *have mercy on us.*
Jesus, mighty God, *have mercy on us.*
Jesus, Father of the world to come, *have mercy on us.*
Jesus, angel of great counsel, *have mercy on us.*
Jesus, most powerful, *have mercy on us.*
Jesus, most patient, *have mercy on us.*
Jesus, most obedient, *have mercy on us.*
Jesus, meek and humble, *have mercy on us.*
Jesus, lover of chastity, *have mercy on us.*
Jesus, lover of us, *have mercy on us.*
Jesus, God of peace, *have mercy on us.*
Jesus, author of life, *have mercy on us.*
Jesus, model of virtues, *have mercy on us.*
Jesus, lover of souls, *have mercy on us.*
Jesus, our God, *have mercy on us.*

Jesus, our refuge, *have mercy on us.*
Jesus, Father of the poor, *have mercy on us.*
Jesus, treasure of the faithful, *have mercy on us.*
Jesus, Good Shepherd, *have mercy on us.*
Jesus, true light, *have mercy on us.*
Jesus, eternal wisdom, *have mercy on us.*
Jesus, infinite goodness, *have mercy on us.*
Jesus, our way and our life, *have mercy on us.*
Jesus, joy of angels, *have mercy on us.*
Jesus, King of patriarchs, *have mercy on us.*
Jesus, master of Apostles, *have mercy on us.*
Jesus, teacher of Evangelists, *have mercy on us.*
Jesus, strength of martyrs, *have mercy on us.*
Jesus, light of confessors, *have mercy on us.*
Jesus, purity of virgins, *have mercy on us.*
Jesus, crown of all saints, *have mercy on us.*

Be merciful, *spare us, O Jesus.*
Be merciful, *graciously hear us, O Jesus.*

From all evil, *Jesus, deliver us.*
From all sin, *Jesus, deliver us.*
From Thy wrath, *Jesus, deliver us.*
From the snares of the devil, *Jesus, deliver us.*
From the spirit of fornication, *Jesus, deliver us.*
From everlasting death, *Jesus, deliver us.*
From the neglect of Thine inspirations, *Jesus, deliver us.*

Through the mystery of Thy holy Incarnation, *Jesus, deliver us.*
Through Thy nativity, *Jesus, deliver us.*
Through Thine infancy, *Jesus, deliver us.*
Through Thy most divine life, *Jesus, deliver us.*
Through Thy labors, *Jesus, deliver us.*
Through Thine agony and Passion, *Jesus, deliver us.*
Through Thy cross and dereliction, *Jesus, deliver us.*
Through Thy sufferings, *Jesus, deliver us.*
Through Thy death and burial, *Jesus, deliver us.*
Through Thy Resurrection, *Jesus, deliver us.*

Through Thine Ascension, *Jesus, deliver us.*
Through Thine institution of the most Holy Eucharist, *Jesus, deliver us.*
Through Thy joys, *Jesus, deliver us.*
Through Thy glory, *Jesus, deliver us.*

Lamb of God, Who takest away the sins of the world, *Spare us, O Jesus.*
Lamb of God, Who takest away the sins of the world, *Graciously hear us, O Jesus.*
Lamb of God, Who takest away the sins of the world, *Have mercy on us.*

Jesus, hear us, *Jesus, graciously hear us.*

Let Us Pray. O Lord Jesus Christ, Who hast said: Ask and ye shall receive, seek and ye shall find, knock and it shall be opened unto you; grant, we beseech Thee, to us who ask the gift of Thy divine love, that we may ever love Thee with all our hearts, and in all our words and actions, and never cease from praising Thee.

Give us, O Lord, a perpetual fear and love of Thy holy Name; for Thou never failest to govern those whom Thou dost solidly establish in Thy love, Who livest and reignest world without end. R. Amen.

ST. LOUIS DE MONTFORT'S PRAYER TO MARY

Hail Mary, beloved Daughter of the Eternal Father! Hail Mary, admirable Mother of the Son! Hail Mary, faithful spouse of the Holy Ghost! Hail Mary, my dear Mother, my loving Mistress, my powerful sovereign! Hail my joy, my glory, my heart and my soul! You are all mine by mercy, and I am all yours by justice. But I am not yet sufficiently yours. I now give myself wholly to you without keeping anything back for myself or others. If you still see in me anything which does not belong to you, I beg you to take it and to make yourself the absolute Mistress of all that is mine. Destroy in me all that may be displeasing to God, root it up and bring it to nothing; place and cultivate in me everything that is pleasing to you.

May the light of your faith dispel the darkness of my mind; may your profound humility take the place of my pride; may your sublime contemplation check the distractions of my wandering imagination; may your continuous sight of God fill my memory with His presence; may the burning love of your heart inflame the lukewarmness of mine; may your virtues take the place of my sins; may your merits be my only adornment in the sight of God and make up for all that is wanting in me. Finally, dearly beloved Mother, grant, if it be possible, that I may have no other spirit but yours to know Jesus and His divine will; that I may have no other soul but yours to praise and glorify the Lord; that I may have no other heart but yours to love God with a love as pure and ardent as yours.

I do not ask you for visions, revelations, sensible devotion or spiritual pleasures. It is your privilege to see God clearly. It is your privilege to enjoy heavenly bliss. It is your privilege to triumph gloriously in Heaven at the right hand of your Son and to hold absolute sway over angels, men and demons. It is your privilege to dispose of all the gifts of God, just as you will.

Such is, O heavenly Mary, the "best part," which the Lord has given you and which shall never be taken away from you, and this thought fills my heart with joy. As for my part here below, I wish for nothing more than that which was yours: to believe sincerely without spiritual pleasures; to suffer joyfully without human consolation; to die continually to myself without respite; and to work zealously and unselfishly for you until death as the humblest of your servants.

The only grace I beg you to obtain for me is that every day and every moment of my life I may say: Amen, so be it, to all that you did while on earth; Amen, so be it, to all you are now doing in Heaven; Amen, so be it, to all that you are doing in my soul, so that you alone may fully glorify Jesus in me for time and eternity. Amen.

O JESUS LIVING IN MARY

O Jesus living in Mary,
Come and live in Thy servants,
In the spirit of Thy holiness,
In the fullness of Thy might,
In the truth of Thy virtues,
In the perfection of Thy ways,
In the communion of Thy mysteries;
Subdue every hostile power
In Thy spirit, for the glory of the Father. Amen.

Appendix II: How-To Guide for Reciting the Rosary

HOW TO PRAY THE ROSARY

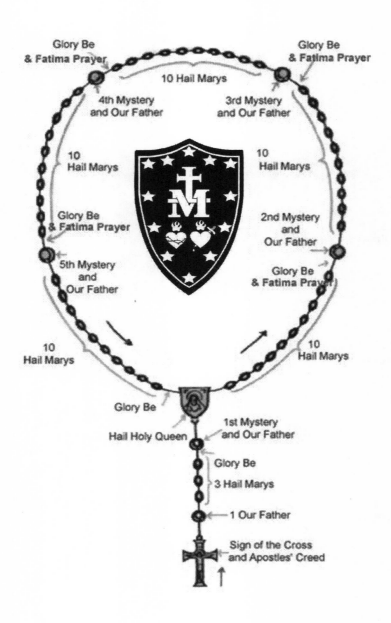

Glory Be & Fatima Prayer

Glory Be & Fatima Prayer

10 Hail Marys

4th Mystery and Our Father

3rd Mystery and Our Father

10 Hail Marys

10 Hail Marys

Glory Be & Fatima Prayer

2nd Mystery and Our Father

5th Mystery and Our Father

Glory Be & Fatima Prayer

10 Hail Marys

10 Hail Marys

Glory Be

1st Mystery and Our Father

Hail Holy Queen

Glory Be

3 Hail Marys

1 Our Father

Sign of the Cross and Apostles' Creed

PRAYERS RECITED WITH ROSARY

The "Apostles' Creed"
I believe in God, the Father Almighty, Creator of heaven and earth; and in Jesus Christ, His only Son, our Lord; Who was conceived by the Holy Spirit, born of the Virgin Mary, suffered under Pontius Pilate, was crucified, died, and was buried. He descended into hell; the third day He arose again from the dead. He ascended into heaven, and sits at the right hand of God, the Father Almighty; from thence He shall come to judge the living and the dead. **I believe in the Holy Spirit, the Holy Catholic Church, the communion of Saints, the forgiveness of sins, the resurrection of the body and life everlasting. Amen.**

Announce the Mystery before beginning the "Our Father (see next section):

The "Our Father"
Our Father, Who art in heaven, hallowed be Thy name; Thy kingdom come; Thy will be done on earth as it is in heaven.
**Give us this day our daily bread;
and forgive us our trespasses
as we forgive those who trespass against us;
and lead us not into temptation,
but deliver us from evil. Amen.**

The "Hail Mary"
Hail Mary, full of grace, the Lord is with thee; blessed art thou among women, and blessed is the fruit of thy womb, Jesus. **Holy Mary, Mother of God, pray for us sinners, now and at the hour of our death. Amen.**

The "Glory Be"

Glory be to the Father,
and to the Son,
and to the Holy Spirit,
**as it was in the beginning,
is now, and ever shall be,
world without end. Amen.**

After each Decade (following the "Glory Be"):

The Prayer Requested by the Blessed Virgin Mary at Fatima
O my Jesus, forgive us our sins, save us from the fires of hell, lead all souls to Heaven, especially those who have most need of your mercy.

After the Rosary:

The "Hail, Holy Queen" (Or *Salve Regina*)
HAIL, HOLY QUEEN, Mother of Mercy, our life, our sweetness and our hope! To thee do we cry, poor banished children of Eve; to thee do we send up our sighs, mourning and weeping in this vale of tears. Turn then, most gracious advocate, thine eyes of mercy toward us, and after this our exile, show unto us the blessed fruit of thy womb, Jesus. O clement, O loving, O sweet Virgin Mary!

> V. Pray for us, O Holy Mother of God.
> R. That we may be made worthy of the promises of Christ.

Let us pray. O GOD, whose only begotten Son, by His life, death, and resurrection, has purchased for us the rewards of eternal life, grant, we beseech Thee, that meditating upon these mysteries of the Most Holy Rosary of the Blessed Virgin Mary, we may imitate what they contain and obtain what they promise, through the same Christ Our Lord. Amen.

Prayer to St. Joseph (optional)

Introduction

This prayer to Saint Joseph—spouse of the Virgin Mary, foster father of Jesus, and patron saint of the universal Church—was composed by Pope Leo XIII in his 1889 encyclical, *Quamquam Pluries*. . . . He asked that it be added to the end of the Rosary, especially during the month of October, which is dedicated to the Rosary. The prayer is enriched with a partial indulgence (*Handbook of Indulgences*, conc. 19), and may be said after the customary *Salve Regina* ("Hail, Holy Queen") and concluding prayer. It may also be used to conclude other Marian devotions.

Prayer
To you, O blessed Joseph,
do we come in our tribulation,
and having implored the help of your most holy Spouse,
we confidently invoke your patronage also.

Through that charity which bound you
to the Immaculate Virgin Mother of God
and through the paternal love
with which you embraced the Child Jesus,
we humbly beg you graciously to regard the inheritance
which Jesus Christ has purchased by his Blood,
and with your power and strength to aid us in our necessities.
O most watchful guardian of the Holy Family,
defend the chosen children of Jesus Christ;
O most loving father, ward off from us
every contagion of error and corrupting influence;
O our most mighty protector, be kind to us
and from heaven assist us in our struggle
with the power of darkness.

As once you rescued the Child Jesus from deadly peril,
so now protect God's Holy Church
from the snares of the enemy and from all adversity;
shield, too, each one of us by your constant protection,
so that, supported by your example and your aid,
we may be able to live piously, to die in holiness,
and to obtain eternal happiness in heaven. Amen.

MYSTERIES OF THE ROSARY

As suggested by the Pope St. John Paul the Great, the Joyful mysteries are said on Monday and Saturday, the Luminous on Thursday, the Sorrowful on Tuesday and Friday, and the Glorious on Wednesday and Sunday (with this exception: Sundays of Christmas season - The Joyful; Sundays of Lent - Sorrowful). See below for the full listing of the different sets of mysteries.

Joyful Mysteries	Monday	Saturday
Sorrowful	Tuesday	Friday
Glorious	Wednesday	Sunday
Luminous	Thursday	

The **Five Joyful Mysteries** are traditionally prayed on the Mondays, Saturdays, and Sundays of Advent:
1. The Annunciation
2. The Visitation
3. The Nativity
4. The Presentation in the Temple
5. The Finding in the Temple

The **Five Sorrowful Mysteries** are traditionally prayed on the Tuesdays, Fridays, and Sundays of Lent:
1. The Agony in the Garden
2. The Scourging at the Pillar
3. The Crowning with Thorns
4. The Carrying of the Cross
5. The Crucifixion and Death

The **Five Glorious Mysteries** are traditionally prayed on the Wednesday and Sundays outside of Lent and Advent:
1. The Resurrection
2. The Ascension

3. The Descent of the Holy Spirit
4. The Assumption
5. The Coronation of Mary

The **Five Luminous Mysteries** are traditionally prayed on Thursdays:
1. The Baptism of Christ in the Jordan
2. The Wedding Feast at Cana
3. Jesus' Proclamation of the Coming of the Kingdom of God
4. The Transfiguration
5. The Institution of the Eucharist

ROSARY PRAYERS IN SPANISH

Sign of the Cross
En el nombre del Padre, y del Hijo, y del Espíritu Santo. Amen.

Apostles Creed
Creo en Dios, Padre todopoderoso, creador del Cielo y de la Tierra. Creo en Jesucristo su único Hijo, Nuestro Señor, que fue concebido por obra y gracia del Espíritu Santo; nació de Santa María Virgen; padeció bajo el poder de Poncio Pilato; fue crucificado, muerto y sepultado; descendió a los infiernos; al tercer día resucitó de entre los muertos; subió a los cielos y está a la diestra de Dios Padre; desde allí ha de venir a juzgar a los vivos y a los muertos. Creo en el Espíritu Santo, en la Santa Iglesia Católica, la comumión de los Santos en el perdon de los pecados la resurrección de los muertos y la vida eterna. Amen.

Our Father
Padre nuestro, que estás en el cielo. Santificado sea tu nombre. Venga tu reino. Hágase tu voluntad en la tierra como

en el cielo. Danos hoy nuestro pan de cada día. Perdona nuestras ofensas, como también nosotros perdonamos a los que nos ofenden. No nos dejes caer en tentación y líbranos del mal. Amen.

Hail Mary
Dios te salve, María. Llena eres de gracia: El Señor es contigo. Bendita tú eres entre todas las mujeres. Y bendito es el fruto de tu vientre: Jesús. Santa María, Madre de Dios, ruega por nosotros pecadores, ahora y en la hora de nuestra muerte. Amen.

Glory Be
Gloria al Padre, al Hijo y al Espíritu Santo. Como era en el principio, ahora y siempre, por los siglos de los siglos. Amen.

Oh My Jesus
Oh mi Jesús, perdónanos nuestros pecados, líbranos del fuego del infierno, lleva todas las almas al cielo, especialmente las mas necesitadas de tu misericordia. Amen.

Hail Holy Queen
Dios te salve, Reina y Madre de misericordia, vida, dulzura y esperanza nuestra, Dios te salve. A ti clamamos los desterrados hijos de Eva. A ti suspiramos gimiendo y llorando en este valle de lágrimas. Ea, pues, Señora, abogada nuestra: vuelve a nosotros esos tus ojos misericordiosos. Y después de este destierro, muéstranos a Jesús, fruto bendito de tu vientre. Oh clemente, oh piadosa, oh dulce Virgen María. Ruega por nosotros, Santa Madre de Dios, para que seamos dignos de las promesas de Cristo. Amen.

Final Prayer
Oh Dios de quién Único Hijo nos ha otorgado los beneficios de la vida eterna, concédenos la gracia que te pedimos mientras meditamos los Misterios del Mas Santo Rosario de la Bienaventurada Virgen María, debemos imitar lo que contienen y obtener lo que prometen, a través del mismo Cristo Nuestro Señor. Amen.

About Scott Smith

Scott Smith is an author, attorney, and theologian from Louisiana. Scott is a lover of all things Catholic: the Eucharist, the Blessed Mother, and especially the King of Kings, Who is the hidden connection between all history, Scripture, culture, and theology.

Check out more of his writing and courses below ...

More from Scott Smith

Scott regularly contributes to his blog, The Scott Smith Blog at www.thescottsmithblog.com, WINNER of the 2018-2019 Fisher's Net Award for Best Catholic Blog:

Scott's other books can be found at his publisher's, Holy Water Books, website, holywaterbooks.com, as well as on Amazon

His other books on theology and the Catholic faith include *The Catholic ManBook, Everything You Need to Know About Mary But Were Never Taught*, and *Blessed is He Who ...* (Biographies of Blesseds). More on these below ...

His fiction includes *The Seventh Word*, a pro-life horror novel, and the *Cajun Zombie Chronicles*, the Catholic version of the zombie apocalypse.

ALL
SAINTS
UNIVERSITY
EST. MMXVII

Scott has also produced courses on the Blessed Mother and Scripture for All Saints University.

Learn about the Blessed Mary from anywhere and learn to defend your mother! It includes over six hours of video plus a free copy of the next book ... Enroll Now!

What You *Need* to Know About Mary But Were Never Taught

Give a robust defense of the Blessed Mother using Scripture. Now, more than ever, every Catholic needs to learn how to defend their mother, the Blessed Mother. Because now, more than ever, the family is under attack and needs its Mother.

Discover the love story, hidden within the whole of Scripture, of the Father for his daughter, the Holy Spirit for his spouse, and the Son for his MOTHER.

This collection of essays and the All Saints University course made to accompany it will demonstrate through Scripture how the Immaculate Conception of Mary was prophesied in Genesis and how the Virgin Mary is the New Eve, the New Ark, and the New Queen of Israel.

ENROLL in the full course now!

Catholic Nerds Podcast

Scott is obviously well-credentialed as a nerd. Check out Scott's podcast: the Catholic Nerds Podcast on iTunes, Podbean, Google Play, and wherever good podcasts are found!

The Catholic ManBook

Do you want to reach Catholic Man LEVEL: EXPERT? *The Catholic ManBook* is your handbook to achieving Sainthood, manly Sainthood. Find the following resources inside, plus many others:

- Top Catholic Apps, Websites, and Blogs
- Everything you need to pray the Rosary
- The Most Effective Daily Prayers & Novenas, including the Emergency Novena
- Going to Confession and Eucharistic Adoration like a boss!
- Mastering the Catholic Liturgical Calendar

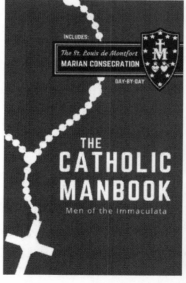

The Catholic ManBook contains the collective wisdom of The Men of the Immaculata, of saints, priests and laymen, fathers and sons, single and married. Holiness is at your fingertips. Get your copy today.

NEW! This year's edition also includes a revised and updated St. Louis de Montfort Marian consecration. Follow the prayers in a day-by-day format.

Blessed is He Who ... Models of Catholic Manhood

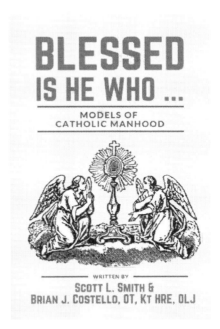

You are the average of the five people you spend the most time with, so spend more time with the Saints! Here are several men that you need to get to know whatever your age or station in life. These short biographies will give you an insight into how to live better, however you're living.

From Kings to computer nerds, old married couples to single teenagers, these men gave us extraordinary examples of holiness:

- Pier Giorgio Frassati & Carlo Acutis – Here are two ex-traordinary **young men**, an athlete and a computer nerd, living on either side of the 20th Century
- Two men of royal stock, Francesco II and Archduke Eu-gen, lived lives of holiness despite all the world conspir-ing against them.

- There's also the **simple husband and father**, Blessed Luigi. Though he wasn't a king, he can help all of us treat the women in our lives as queens.

Blessed Is He Who … Models of Catholic Manhood explores the lives of six men who found their greatness in Christ and His Bride, the Church.

In six succinct chapters, the authors, noted historian Brian J. Costello and theologian and attorney Scott L. Smith, share with you the uncommon lives of exceptional men who will one day be numbered among the Saints of Heaven, men who can bring all of us closer to sainthood.

THANKS FOR READING!
TOTUS TUUS

Made in the USA
Middletown, DE
05 October 2022

12012565R00116